The Development Dimension

Innovation for Water Infrastructure Development in the Mekong Region

Please cite this publication as:
OECD/ADBI/Mekong Institute (2020), *Innovation for Water Infrastructure Development in the Mekong Region*, The Development Dimension, OECD Publishing, Paris, *https://doi.org/10.1787/167498ea-en*.

ISBN 978-92-64-81904-7 (print)
ISBN 978-92-64-90245-9 (pdf)

The Development Dimension
ISSN 1990-1380 (print)
ISSN 1990-1372 (online)

Photo credits: Cover design by Aida Buendía (OECD Development Centre) on the basis of an image from © Macrovector/Shutterstock.com.

Corrigenda to publications may be found on line at: *www.oecd.org/about/publishing/corrigenda.htm*.

Foreword

Expanding access to clean reliable water sources entails a number of direct and indirect economic benefits. Clean reliable water supplies strengthen human capital by improving both health and economic outcomes, and attracting human migration and commerce. According to the latest edition of the *Economic Outlook for Southeast Asia, China and India*, demand for clean water supply and infrastructure remains high throughout the region, and has become an even greater concern in times of COVID-19. Difficulty accessing clean, reliable water means that COVID-19 can spread more easily, with potentially deadly consequences.

Innovation for Water Infrastructure Development in the Mekong Region, jointly produced by the OECD Development Centre, the Asian Development Bank Institute (ADBI) and the Mekong Institute, aims at providing relevant analysis and recommendations for policy makers working to improve water-related infrastructure in the region. This publication covers five main topics, addressing the challenges faced by policy makers, and providing a global perspective through references to case studies outside the Mekong region. The five main topics are: the socio-economic benefits and environmental challenges of the Mekong River; the potential of digital infrastructure financing, with a focus on Fintech and blockchain; the merits of generating private financing for water supply and inland water transport, using spillover tax revenues; the resilience of water infrastructure to natural disasters and COVID-19; the challenges of water regulation in the Mekong region.

The Mekong River spans five countries and is the backbone of several ecosystems and societies along its course. Therefore, pollution, anthropogenic environmental changes and climate change are critical threats that must be addressed collectively among the Mekong River Basin economies. From a financial point of view, a large part of funding for Mekong River Basin infrastructure projects comes from public coffers; however to bring vital projects to fruition, there is a need for more private participation. This is especially true under the COVID-19 pandemic, as state finances across the globe have been heavily strained, with a sharp decline in incoming tax revenues coinciding with a need to disburse public funds. Digital tools, such as Fintech and blockchain, can be leveraged to promote private contributions, and arrangements that enable private investors to recover funds through spillover tax revenues could potentially make the return on investment worthwhile. Efforts in improving water infrastructure resilience to natural disasters can follow two complementary approaches: on one hand, promoting multi-purpose and nature-based solutions to improve hard infrastructure, and on the other, institutional collaboration and community engagement to strengthen soft infrastructure. Finally, the publication examines the challenges facing water regulation. Several issues need to be addressed: tariffs are currently too low to cover operation and maintenance, and collection is ineffective. Water quality oversight can be weak, infrequent, and even absent in some countries. In cases where strong regulations do exist, they can still be undermined by weak enforcement. Horizontal and vertical intergovernmental communication as well as bilateral communication among officials and the public are essential for resolving these issues.

The OECD Development Centre is committed to working alongside the governments of developing and emerging economies and regional actors to identify and address challenges in infrastructure investment and other policy areas. The Centre enjoys full membership of two Mekong region countries: Thailand and Viet Nam. We hope that this report, through its rigorous analysis, peer learning and sharing of best practices, will highlight the importance of investing in water-related infrastructure and contribute to discussions on its role in the region's development.

Acknowledgements

Innovation for Water Infrastructure Development in the Mekong Region was prepared by the Asia Desk of the OECD Development Centre, in collaboration with the Asian Development Bank Institute (ADBI) and Mekong Institute. The team was led by Kensuke Tanaka, Head of Asia Desk and Prasiwi Ibrahim, Deputy Head of Asia Desk, OECD Development Centre, in co-operation with Naoyuki Yoshino, Dean of ADBI (at the time of preparing the report) and Watcharas Leelawath, Executive Director of the Mekong Institute. Valuable guidance was provided by Mario Pezzini, Director of the OECD Development Centre and Special Advisor to the OECD Secretary-General on Development.

This publication was prepared by a core team composed of Kensuke Tanaka, Prasiwi Ibrahim, Ryan Jacildo and Rahmalia Devita at the OECD Development Centre (Chapters 2, 4 and 5); Naoyuki Yoshino at the ADBI, Masaki Nakahigashi, and Umid Abidhadjaev (Chapter 3); as well as Watcharas Leelawath and Ratna Devi Nadarajan at the Mekong Institute (Chapter 1). Alexander Hume, Raluca Maran, Isa Mulder, Asia Desk of the OECD Development Centre provided useful inputs and comments. Dasom Kim and Saumya Bhavsar contributed to collection of relevant information. Sonja Marki provided administrative support for this project. Delphine Grandrieux, Elizabeth Nash and Aida Buendia turned the manuscript into a publication.

The publication also benefitted from co-operation and discussions with experts in the region and other international organisations. The intermediate results of this report was presented at the Mekong Forum, in Khon Kaen, Thailand, in July 2019. The authors are grateful to Akhmad Bayhaqi, APEC Policy Support Unit (PSU) and Kettivit Sittisoontornwong, Thai International Freight Forwarders Association (TIFFA) for the valuable inputs.

Support from OECD Delegation, in particular, Yoshifumi Fukunaga, Yuji Nakayama, Toshiki Okabayashi, Masaya Sugimoto, and Nao Takada, is gratefully acknowledged.

Last but not least, the OECD Development Centre is most grateful for the financial support received from the Ministry of Economy, Trade and Industry (METI), Japan.

Table of contents

FIGURES

TABLES

Follow OECD Publications on:

http://twitter.com/OECD_Pubs

http://www.facebook.com/OECDPublications

http://www.linkedin.com/groups/OECD-Publications-4645871

http://www.youtube.com/oecdilibrary

OECD Alerts http://www.oecd.org/oecddirect/

This book has...

StatLinks

A service that delivers Excel® files from the printed page!

Look for the *StatLinks* at the bottom of the tables or graphs in this book. To download the matching Excel® spreadsheet, just type the link into your Internet browser, starting with the ***https://doi.org*** prefix, or click on the link from the e-book edition.

Executive summary

Countries in the Mekong region recorded impressive economic growth in the last decades, mainly due to the economic opportunities provided by the Mekong River, at the same time, they also face multiple challenges. For instance, water infrastructure needs are increasing but private sector participation in water infrastructure remains dismal and options of infrastructure financing are limited. In addition, there remains ample room for improvement of water regulations. Innovative approaches are therefore needed to address these challenges. *Innovation for Water Infrastructure Development in the Mekong Region* covers five main topics: the socio-economic contributions and environmental challenges of the Mekong River (Chapter 1), the potential of digital infrastructure financing, with a focus on Fintech and blockchain (Chapter 2), the merits of inducing private finance to water supply and inland water transport using spillover tax revenues (Chapter 3), the resilience of water infrastructure to natural disasters and COVID-19 (Chapter 4), and the challenges of water regulation in the Mekong region (Chapter 5).

Socio-economic contributions and environmental challenges of the Mekong River

Countries in the Mekong River Basin (MRB) have recorded impressive economic growth, leveraging the development opportunities provided by the Mekong River. Owing to its unique morphological features, the river serves as a lifeline to millions of MRB residents, providing irrigation supply, hydropower, fishery products, and opportunities in navigation, tourism and sediment extraction. However, the MRB is one of the river basins in the world most vulnerable to climate change and failure to adapt behaviour to changing weather patterns could hamper or reverse growth in the region.

Adaptation to climate change for riparian communities in transboundary river basins calls for increased co-operation in terms of regional security and economic development. The level of co-operation is highly influenced by national socio-economic priorities and major uses of transboundary rivers. Future transboundary co-operation in the MRB has a strong foundation on which to build.

Potential of digital infrastructure financing: Fintech and blockchain technology

The private sector is increasingly engaged in financing infrastructure in Asia, primarily through partnerships with the public sector and via privatisation. Notwithstanding, the public sector continues to fund most infrastructure in the region. Alternative finance mechanisms are emerging, however, that harness digital technologies (e.g. Fintech, blockchain tokens) to fund infrastructure. Such platforms, including crowdfunding and tokenisation, can help transcend the limits of traditional banks, providing a lower entry cost for retail investors and sending a reassuring signal to larger institutional investors.

Despite some success stories, the use of crowdfunding and tokenisation to finance public infrastructure is still limited in the region. It is primarily for last-mile needs and is largely donation-based. Nevertheless, progress in using alternative financing schemes to develop real estate or water projects could set the stage for broader usage of these platforms in general public infrastructure financing. Continued growth of Fintech will depend on adequacy of risk assessment, especially for large transactions like infrastructure projects. The availability and depth of secondary markets for transactions is another important factor in broadening the use of alternative platforms.

Inducing private finance to water supply and inland water transport

While the public sector supplies most of the water, private investors could help expand the water network in many parts of countries in the Mekong region. Public-private partnerships have been advocated for many years, but the low returns discourage private sector involvement. Water supply and other infrastructure investments rely on user charges as their main source of revenue. Unless user charges are high enough to cover the costs of construction and operation, the private sector is reluctant to invest in infrastructure.

Infrastructure investment can create huge spillover effects for the economy which will increase regional output and thus increase revenues for the government in terms of various taxes. Past experience has shown, however, that all these incremental tax revenues mainly benefitted governments rather than being returned to water supply companies that relied solely on user charges as source of returns. Water supply thus relied on public money, which restricted its expansion. By partly returning spillover tax revenues to investors, the rate of return from the water supply would increase. This would encourage private investors to invest in water supply.

Resilience of water infrastructure to natural disasters and COVID-19

Countries in the Mekong region are particularly prone to natural disasters such as floods, storms, drought, earthquakes, landslides and epidemics. Climate change, rapid and unplanned urbanisation, as well as environmental degradation, are among factors that increase countries' vulnerability to natural hazards. The COVID-19 outbreak has also demonstrated the need to build resilience in the face of a pandemic. Since these external shocks can lead to significant socio-economic consequences, improving resilience against natural disasters is primordial.

Efforts in this regard can take two complementary approaches. Promoting multi-purpose and nature-based solutions can improve hard infrastructure, while institutional collaboration and community engagement can strengthen soft infrastructure. Joint planning between countries is needed since the impact of water-related hazards is often transboundary. The importance of effective early warning systems also cannot be neglected. Advancements in technology create new possibilities to invent low-cost digital tools for early warning systems. Among digital tools, mobile phone use has gained importance in the region. However, efforts would be needed in reaching remote vulnerable areas.

As countries may face future natural disasters and epidemics, the important role played by proper hygiene in slowing the spread of COVID-19 provides a critical lesson. Countries need to accelerate the development of resilient and sustainable water infrastructure and increase its access. Indeed, this should be a priority in order to ensure that reliable and safe water remains widespread and accessible even during challenging times.

Challenges of water regulation in the Mekong region

Water and wastewater regulators are usually part of a broad regulatory framework at national or sub-national level. The examination of policies and legislation in the five MRB countries reveals that Viet Nam is more advanced in water regulation compared to its regional peers. In general, all five countries seem to lack services for monitoring performance and managing audits on utilities.

In general, several issues may need to be addressed: tariffs that are too low to cover operation and maintenance (O&M) costs, lack of data and limited human resource capacity. This suggests there is scope for improving regulation of the water and wastewater services (WWS) sector in the Mekong countries. Complex challenges such as governance and financial sustainability issues prevail across the MRB countries with respect to accessing water infrastructure. Universal access to safe drinking water, sanitation and hygiene provides both health and economic benefits.

Overview: Innovative approaches to building resilient water infrastructure in the Mekong region

This overview summarises the main points contained in the five chapters of the publication on *Innovation for Water Infrastructure Development in the Mekong Region*. Chapter 1 provides a snapshot of the key socio-economic and environmental challenges facing the Mekong River and underlines the importance of transboundary initiatives to address these challenges. Chapter 2 explores the benefits of innovative financing models enabled by technologies, such as crowdfunding and tokenisation. Chapter 3 analyses infrastructure investment needs and focuses on spillover tax revenues to boost private sector participation. Chapter 4 presents a variety of initiatives that could enhance the resilience of water infrastructure in the face of natural disasters, putting particular emphasis on community engagement and digital tools. Chapter 5 completes the picture with a discussion about the weaknesses of water and wastewater regulations in the Mekong countries and highlights a few priority areas for reform.

The Mekong River is essential for socio-economic development of the region, though challenges need to be addressed

The Mekong River originates about 5 200 metres above sea level at the Tibetan Plateau and discharges into the South China Sea after travelling 4 350 km. The annual economic value of water-related sectors in the Mekong River Basin (MRB) is estimated at almost USD 35 billion, excluding forestry and tourism. The benefits derived from the Mekong River system are multi-dimensional; with social, economic, environmental and other aspects. The river provides irrigation for agriculture, fisheries, transportation, water supply, hydropower, tourism-related opportunities and sediment extraction. Agriculture and irrigation are the major beneficiaries of the Mekong River, using 70% of its water resources. The total irrigated area in the basin is approximately 4 million hectares, and irrigated areas are expanding steadily in four countries (Cambodia, Lao People's Democratic Republic, Thailand, and Viet Nam). Thailand and Viet Nam continue to draw the greatest economic benefits, particularly from agriculture and fisheries, including aquaculture. Lao People's Democratic Republic (hereafter 'Lao PDR') is generating most of its economic benefits from Mekong resources through investment in hydropower. Meanwhile, Cambodia continues to enhance fisheries. However, the countries need to cope with socio-economic and environmental challenges, including those posed by climate change.

Climate change poses risks to the river and the countries in its basin. It could affect water security in the MRB and the life of its inhabitants. The changes of weather patterns affect the agriculture production cycle and fish breeding. Meanwhile, changes in water level and flow affect the navigation route and operation of hydropower plants and reservoirs. The wet season increases vulnerability to floods, while the dry season suggests greater potential for drought periods. Expansion of agriculture in the basin is limited by water availability in the dry season. Climate change also threatens biodiversity in the MRB. As climate change alters water availability, changing rainfall patterns could reduce or change the flow of rivers, threatening the generation potential of hydropower.

Strengthening transboundary co-operation

Due to the transboundary nature of the river, MRB countries need to strengthen co-operation to implement basin-wide climate adaptation measures. Co-operation enables joint development of more cost-effective solutions, which potentially offer benefits to all riparian parties.

MRB countries have implemented a number of projects and programmes through their governments, transboundary co-operation or donor support. These target various sectors, including climate-smart agriculture, green freight, food security, sustainable fisheries and alternative sources of green energy. However, the benefits of co-operation mechanisms in climate adaptation are not widely realised, often due to competing economic interests among the MRB countries and emphasis on using the Mekong River as a water resource.

Innovative approaches are needed to address various new challenges. *Innovation for Water Infrastructure Development in the Mekong Region* covers the topics of digital infrastructure financing, spillover effects of water transport, resilience to natural disasters, and challenges of water regulation, following an overview of socio-economic and environmental challenges.

Digital tools such as Fintech and blockchain technology provide potential for infrastructure financing

Asia, including the Mekong region, has significant financing needs for infrastructure, but has difficulties obtaining suitable financing from sources beyond the public sector (OECD, 2018[1]). The public sector continues to finance the majority of infrastructure in Asia and the Mekong region, although the private sector is increasingly involved through public-private partnerships (PPPs) and privatisation. In total, approximately 70% of Asian infrastructure funding comes directly from the public sector. The private sector contributes 20%, while multilateral agencies, such as international development banks, contribute the rest.

Public sector funding draws on tax and non-tax revenues, as well as borrowing and loans from multilateral institutions. Private sector participation leans more on the debt market, especially bank lending, even though relying on banks to fund infrastructure poses challenges. Since banks' loanable funds are largely composed of demand deposits, the tenor of their investments is limited to shorter periods. Performance and asset quality ratios demanded of banks in a well-supervised environment also limit the volume of loanable capital. Furthermore, traditional lending by banks often gives limited attention to community needs and interests. Equity issuance and corporate bonds of entities directly involved in infrastructure sectors such as utilities, transportation and mining represent other sources of funding. Institutional investors such as sovereign wealth funds, pension funds and insurance companies have increasing interest in infrastructure as an asset, but current policy fails to facilitate this funding mechanism, with investor regulation representing one of the major constraints. The market for securities is also generally at an early stage of development in many countries, therefore opportunities for countries in the region to develop alternative financing mechanisms beyond the public sector are plentiful.

Developing alternative and innovative funding channels

Tools using digital technologies could be potential alternatives. Such platforms can help surpass the limits of traditional banks, providing a lower entry cost for retail investors. They can also indicate community support, sending a reassuring signal to larger institutional investors. Technology-enabled financing platforms have grown significantly in the last few years and become a popular choice for small projects that would have had difficulty obtaining capital from traditional creditors. Crowdfunding and tokenisation are some examples, although the use of these tools to finance public infrastructure remains limited.

Crowdfunding is one way for individuals or participants to pool funds to finance businesses, projects, or other needs of enterprises or individuals. In general, crowdfunding can take the form of debt, equity, royalty, reward or donation. In a crowdfunding system, fundraising mainly involves the investor, the capital recipient or the borrower, and the marketplace platform (Figure 0.1). The link between the investor and the capital recipient is more direct compared to the banking system.

Figure 0.1. Basic crowdfunding model (simplified representation)

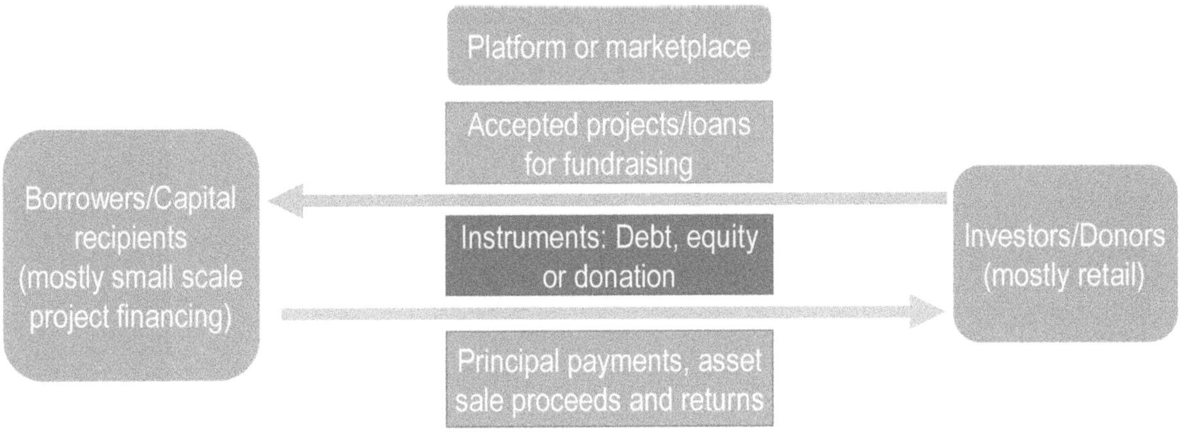

Source: Authors.

Tokenisation is another potential option to raise capital for infrastructure either through debt or equity. Tokenisation lessens reliance on traditional intermediaries in the flow of funding. After government-issued funds (fiat money) are converted into tokens, payment, clearing and settlement would no longer pass through banks, custodians and clearinghouses. This will then lower the cost and financial barriers to investor participation. Tokenisation in the context of infrastructure divides the value of assets or the underlying securities (debt or equity) into smaller parcels before they are offered to potential investors (Figure 0.2). Thus, tokenisation could be used to foster liquidity in an asset market that is typically illiquid, such as real estate. Moreover, tokens carry relatively lower transaction costs than traditional securities; their digital nature makes their usage more efficient, while blockchain technology enhances transparency.

Figure 0.2. Basic tokenisation model (simplified representation)

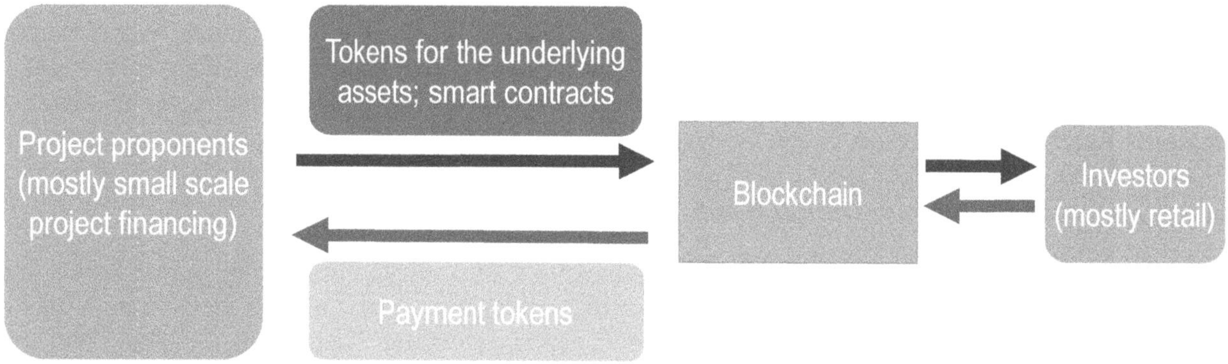

Source: Authors.

Exploring the use of technology-enabled financing platforms

Crowdfunding and blockchain tokens have been used to finance various projects, including those in agriculture, the arts, health, fashion, retail goods and technology. In water-related infrastructure, digital financing based on Fintech and blockchain technology, in particular crowdfunding, has emerged as an important source of funding. It has already been applied in various OECD and Asian countries. Fintech-based finance efforts, in particular, often support the water infrastructure needs of local communities. Table 0.1 highlights some successful examples: 1) the Pitak Project in the Philippines; 2) the water purification project in Branson, Colorado, United States; 3) the project to improve water quality in Buttah Windee, West Australia; 4) the Water for Arubot project in Nepal; and 5) the water vending machine in Ngomai, Tanzania. Strong need expressed by the community, together with transparency and promotion, are some of the key success factors.

Table 0.1. Water infrastructure project case studies (examples)

Project	Location	Infrastructure type	Description
The Pitak Project	Tubao, la Union, Northern Philippines	Deep-well pump, water storage and distribution	A solar-powered deep well with a water storage and distribution system to eliminate dependence on the unreliable local water and electricity supplies.
Water purification	Branson, Colorado, United States	Water filtration system	A water filtration system to bring existing spring water sources into compliance with water quality regulations after authorities raised concerns of surface water contamination.
Hygroscopic water collection	Buttah Windee, Mid-West Region, West Australia, Australia	Alternative water collection system, water storage and distribution	A solar-powered hygroscopic water collection system extracts pure water from air. It replaces water supply contaminated with uranium.
Water for Arubot	Arubot, Kavrepanchok District, Nepal	Collection and storage of water from a nearby river	This project would allow for the use of a nearby river as a dependable water source to ease reliance on rainfall. The project is in the feasibility study stage.
Flint Community Water Lab	Flint, Michigan, United States	Water quality testing laboratory	An independent water-testing laboratory staffed by residents who will be trained for this purpose.
Water Vending Machine	Ngomai, Tanzania	Paid-use water pump	This pump provides clean water to a community and liberates women for other pursuits than water retrieval. Fees cover costs of repairs, done by trained locals.
Diamer-bhasha and Mohmand dams	Pakistan	Dams	These dams will be used to form reservoirs and alleviate water scarcity.

Source: Authors.

Despite some successful examples, the use of crowdfunding and tokenisation to finance public infrastructure in the region is still limited. It is mainly for last-mile needs and largely based on donations. However, progress in using alternative financing to develop projects in real estate, transport, power and water could set the stage for a broader usage of these platforms in general public infrastructure financing in the coming years. Continued growth of Fintech will depend on adequate risk assessment, especially for large transactions like infrastructure projects. The availability and depth of secondary markets for transactions is another important factor in facilitating the use of alternative platforms in an effective manner.

Spillover tax revenues can also be used for inducing private finance to water-related infrastructure

Countries in the region need various kinds of infrastructure investment, including electricity supply, water supply and sewerage. Water is a necessary public good. While the public sector supplies most water, private investors could help expand water networks and thus increase water supply. PPPs have long been discussed as a potential strategy for the sector. However, many countries have struggled to attract the private sector especially due to low returns on such projects. Water supply and many other infrastructure investments rely on user charges as their main source of revenue. Unless user charges are high enough to cover the costs of construction and operation, attracting the private sector to invest in infrastructure is difficult. If returns were high enough, private investors such as insurance companies and pension funds could also finance water supply, sanitation and inland water transport. If private sector involvement were to supplement public sector spending on infrastructure (rather than replacing it), the range of possible infrastructure developments would be expanded. Realisation of some of these possibilities would then lead to economic growth, job creation and mitigation of income disparities.

Attracting private sector investment by using spillover tax revenues

Water infrastructure investments increase productivity, in addition to creating significant spillover effects for the economy. New business opportunities will arise along the water supply, attracting commercial and manufacturing activities as well as tourists. This, in turn, will increase property values and create new employment. A safe and reliable water supply will also improve the health of people in the region, contributing to higher productivity. The externality effects of infrastructure investment are difficult to measure; however, the impact of these effects on the economy will be reflected through increased tax revenues.

Case studies illustrate the spillover effect of infrastructure. The economy of urban and rural areas along the railway in Uzbekistan grew by 2% more than in other regions. This difference was due to the spillover effects after the railway connected the production region to the market, creating substantial tax revenues. In the case of the Star Highway in Manila, tax revenues increased from around PHP 490 billion prior to construction to over PHP 622 billion and PHP 652 billion after construction had started. Tax revenues amounted to PHP 1 208 billion starting with the fourth year, about twice as much compared to the pre-construction period.

In the past, all these incremental tax revenues benefitted governments, while private companies relied solely on user charges for their source of returns. The low returns discouraged private sector involvement in financing water infrastructure projects. Water infrastructure thus relied almost exclusively on public money, which restricted expansion in many countries in Asia. Partly returning spillover tax revenues to investors would increase the rate of return. This, in turn, would provide private investors with an incentive to invest in the project. If part of the increased tax revenues were returned to water transport businesses, user charges could be kept low. Furthermore, spillover tax revenues will create additional revenues for the port authority, supplementing user charges. The port authority can invest these revenues into continued economic development, either through new projects or the maintenance of existing ones.

Water infrastructure, including water supply and inland water transport, will have a bigger economic impact in regions with larger population densities. Rural regions may not be able to create such sizeable spillover effects and the incremental tax revenues might be smaller. The government can therefore set up a cap for private investors. This means that if the total rate of return (part of spillover tax revenues and user charges) surpasses the cap, the government would take the remainder of increased tax revenues and use them to develop and enhance water supply to rural regions.

Water infrastructure resilience to natural disasters must improve

Natural disasters can slow or reverse development by destroying infrastructure and other forms of physical capital. The impact of natural disasters on water infrastructure can drive communities back into difficulties, especially in areas where the economy relies heavily on agriculture. Damage to water infrastructure caused by natural hazards may contaminate water and disrupt service provision, leaving communities with unsafe and unreliable water supplies. This can increase the exposure of communities to water-borne diseases, especially during flood events. In addition, environmental degradation due to human overexploitation can reduce the capacity of ecosystems to protect against natural hazards, thus increasing vulnerability to disasters. Multi-purpose infrastructure, including nature-based solutions, as well as community-based disaster risk management may help improve resilience against natural hazards, although a number of challenges remain to be addressed. Water infrastructure resiliency became a foremost concern during the recent COVID-19 outbreak due to the necessity of access to clean water to maintain health and prevent the spread of disease.

Adapting to natural disasters with multi-purpose water infrastructure

With the increasing risk of exposure to natural disasters, conventional water infrastructure – often single-purpose and with limited capacity in terms of disaster mitigation – is becoming more vulnerable to natural hazards. Multi-purpose water infrastructure projects that address economic, social and environmental concerns may help. In Mekong countries, multi-purpose water infrastructure is still rare. Multi-purpose dams account for only 1% of total dams in the Mekong basin (Cambodia, Lao PDR, Thailand and Viet Nam). A single-purpose dam is often more financially attractive for private investors, as it has lower risks and secure financial returns on the energy produced. Thus, financing for multi-purpose dams often comes almost exclusively from public resources. The lack of joint planning between border provinces is another challenge to resilient water infrastructure development in the region.

Strengthening urban resilience with nature-based solutions

Interventions in ecosystems inspired and supported by nature (nature-based solutions or NBS), have often been considered as complements or even substitutes to conventional infrastructure. This concept may offer effective and low-cost solutions to increase resilience, while delivering other benefits such as biodiversity, air quality or even possibilities for recreational activities. NBS can also be implemented to achieve water-related objectives, such as wetlands restoration for improving water resource management and boosting resilience against water-related hazards. A type of NBS called water-sensitive urban design (WSUD) may gain importance as cities become more vulnerable to the effects of environmental degradation and disasters induced by climate change. WSUD tools are flexible enough to be integrated into any type of urban development, such as building units, parks and other open spaces with waterways. The concept may thus offer solutions for cities to become more resilient and liveable, while providing vibrant spaces for communities. As the concept is relatively new for most developing cities in Mekong countries, strong commitment and political leadership, as well as community engagement, may be needed.

Using community-based solutions for better disaster resilience

Resilience against natural hazards may also depend on institutional capacity to prepare for disasters. Fragmented sectoral approaches and institutional arrangements could render the implementation of disaster risk management more difficult. Lack of information and technical skills to execute plans are additional challenges that hinder disaster preparedness. It is also crucial that communities are engaged as community-led co-ordinating mechanisms are often cost-effective since local needs and circumstances can be addressed properly.

Cambodia

The National Committee for Disaster Management is the main government structure in terms of co-ordinating actions related to disaster risk reduction (DRR). The country has implemented several community-based programmes. However, limited resources and information sharing with all levels of the government sector may hinder the effectiveness of the programmes. A project for flood risk reduction is an example of a community-based solution in the Takeo province of Cambodia. One of its activities consists of helping the most vulnerable families to build elevated houses; their small bamboo homes are prone to damage by heavy rains, flooding and strong winds. Similar community-based projects may offer an effective approach for training and capacity building at the community level elsewhere throughout the country.

Lao PDR

Community-based DRR programmes in Lao PDR are implemented through the Village Disaster Prevention Units and the Village Disaster Prevention and Control Committees. They aim to increase awareness among local communities, enabling them to learn actions to be taken before, during and after disasters. The objective of the School Flood Safety Programs, for example, is to enhance the capacity of communities to cope with floods. These programs operate in communities most at risk of flooding. Due to uneven implementation of the DRR strategy across the country, the capacity to manage the risk of disasters varies at the local level. Improving co-ordination and resource allocation from the central level may help meet the challenge.

Myanmar

Myanmar's 2017 Action Plan on Disaster Risk Reduction acknowledges community-based disaster resilience as a priority action. Since the concept of DRR is relatively new in Myanmar, programmes related to community-based DRR are still limited. Moreover, inadequate financial resources along with lack of institutional arrangement at district or village level have contributed to uneven distribution of community-based DRR programmes. Drought-resilient farming in the dry zone of Myanmar is an example of fruitful DRR in the country. It introduced participatory drought-resistant rice varietal selection in 2014 to strengthen the resilience of subsistence agriculture in this area. Furthermore, access to a wider variety of drought-resilient crops is made possible thanks to the community-level seed banks.

Thailand

Community-based disaster risk management is one of the country's strategies to improve preparations for mitigating the effects of natural hazards. Despite the relatively solid implementation of the DRR strategy at the national, provincial and community level, the lack of risk information and data sharing hampers the ability of governments to make informed decisions on DRR measures. Further capacity building on the use of technology for government officials, community members and other stakeholders is needed. Several community-based measures have been developed at different localities, such as innovative water solutions in Limthong. For this community, extreme drought during the dry season and severe flooding during the rainy season are the main challenges. The Community Water Resource Management (CWRM) concept was introduced to allow knowledge and technology transfers between villagers and other stakeholders, enabling them to better develop and implement appropriate DRR solutions.

Viet Nam

In Viet Nam, while some projects that adopt top-down approaches might not address local resilience effectively, bottom-up approaches of community-based disaster risk management have shown effectiveness in increasing community awareness. Degradation of the mangrove forest has been a major challenge for Da Loc and Nga Thuy communes. Many DRR projects took place in the area, but local participation was limited. In 2007, a community-based approach for strengthening coastal resilience was introduced. As an institutional output, a Community-Based Mangrove Management Board (CMMB) was formed. With strong support from the local government, the CMMB has mobilised community members to effectively contribute to mangrove restoration and disaster preparedness planning.

Maximising the use of digital tools as an effective early warning system

Advancements in technology create new possibilities to develop low-cost digital tools for early warning systems. These tools could offer better quality and timeliness in transferring information, analysis, monitoring, assessing risk and forecasting, thus allowing better awareness and preparedness against disasters. However, developing countries have a large technological gap in the use of such systems compared to developed countries.

Mobile phones have gained importance in developing countries. In fact, each country in the Mekong region has developed its own early warning phone service. Cambodia has the EWS1294; Myanmar owns a mobile phone application called *Disaster Alert Notification*; and Thailand brought forward an initiative called *Warning Volunteer Networking* or *Mr. Warning*. Early warning systems can also be found in several coastal provinces in Viet Nam. While Lao PDR's SMS warning system is still in its initial stages, a pilot project has been underway since early 2019. However, despite improvements within the country, the lack of a national early warning system remains an issue.

Addressing water challenges amid the COVID-19 pandemic

More recently, COVID-19 has been rapidly spreading across the globe. The outbreak highlights the importance of safe and reliable water supply since frequent hand-washing is the most recommended measure to minimise the spread of the virus (OECD, 2020[2]). However, a certain percentage of the population in the region still lacks adequate access to hand-washing facilities with soap and water (Figure 0.3). Improving access to drinking water also remains a challenge, especially for Cambodia, Lao PDR and Myanmar.

Within an urban setting, people living in densely populated areas, especially informal settlements, can also be at greater risk during the COVID-19 and other potential outbreaks. In these areas, physical distancing is nearly impossible, especially at communal water points and sanitation facilities (mostly open pit latrines) where queues often form. These settlements are often not connected to basic services such as piped water, sanitation facilities, and networks for drainage and water treatment. Furthermore, limited household budgets make it difficult to afford access to safe water, and the job losses and economic hardship brought about by the pandemic only serve to exacerbate this issue.

Besides water and sanitation challenges, people living in informal settlements are particularly susceptible to the risk of flooding on a near-daily basis; their settlements are located along rivers, on swamp land or on the riverbed. Disaster preparedness and response plans are often absent, making them even more vulnerable to the effects of flooding. Living conditions, along with daily flooding and other natural hazards, increase the prevalence of vector- and water-borne diseases such as diarrhoea, dysentery, malaria and tuberculosis. These diseases, in turn, reduce immunity and increase the risk of exposure to COVID-19. Thus, addressing unequal access to water is therefore necessary, particularly in densely-populated urban areas.

Figure 0.3. Population using a hand-washing facility with soap and water (percentage), 2017

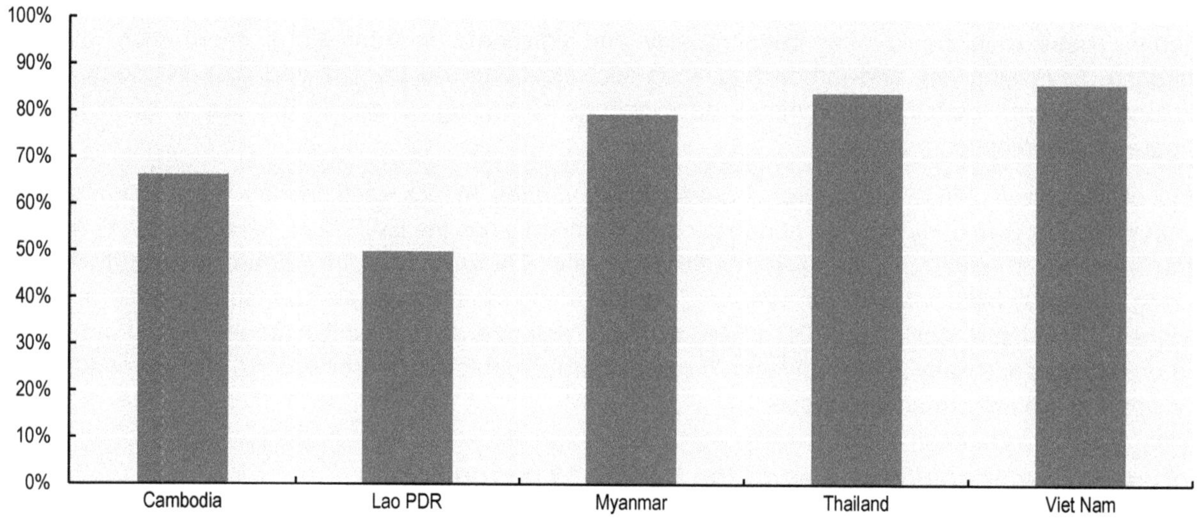

StatLink https://doi.org/10.1787/888934167714

Source: WHO-UNICEF (2020[3]), Joint Monitoring Programme for Water Supply, Sanitation and Hygiene (database), https://sdg6data.org/tables.

The COVID-19 outbreak has also affected large-scale infrastructure projects, especially hydropower dam projects along the Mekong River and its tributaries. These projects are at risk of delays and shutdowns due to lockdowns, movement restrictions and fear of contracting the virus among workers. Meanwhile, small-scale projects with dual objectives are emerging. They aim to increase disaster resilience, while dealing with the socio-economic impact of the COVID-19 outbreak.

Apart from infrastructure, information regarding guidelines on ensuring safety during the crisis must be disseminated to all communities, especially those not connected to piped water systems and who need to buy water. Mobile phones can also play an important part in raising community awareness and facilitating COVID-19 risk communication. Community leaders may also play an important role in strengthening compliance with basic preventive measures to be applied in other activities that require close contact between people.

Some challenges remain to be addressed in water regulations in the Mekong region

Universal access to safe drinking water, sanitation and hygiene benefits health, well-being, the economy and the environment. However, the Mekong region faces a number of challenges in these areas. In addition to the need for more financing, co-ordination among actors should improve. Water and wastewater regulators are usually part of a broad regulatory framework at national or sub-national level. These involve different line ministries, local authorities and non-governmental bodies such as consumer advocacy groups or associations of utility professionals. Ensuring strong co-ordination among the different actors is crucial for a smooth implementation of water infrastructure projects.

The water and wastewater services (WWS) sector has several common characteristics and regulators could therefore play a role in ensuring effective water regulations. These include addressing "market failures" in WWS so the sector can fully meet the public interest for all stakeholders at the least cost; promoting easy and transparent access to data; balancing the economic, social and environmental aspects of WWS; ensuring delivery in accordance with the principle of universality, continuity, quality of services, equality of access, affordability and transparency; setting quality standards for drinking water and wastewater treatment to protect public health; and enhancing co-ordination among actors.

Enhancing water and wastewater services regulations in Mekong countries

In the Mekong region, WWS regulations could be much improved, but some challenges remain. Financial sustainability is needed in water tariff regulation. Quality standards for drinking water should be strengthened and laws for wastewater treatment enforced. The region needs to address public service obligations and social regulation, define standards of technical modalities and service delivery, and identify and prevent risk to water availability. Further, it needs to provide incentives in agriculture for more efficient water use, improve private sector involvement, promote innovative technologies through PPP and facilitate initiatives to reduce water demand. It also needs to analyse the investment plans of water utilities, improve information gathering and data collection, and develop the capacity of water operators. Finally, it should strengthen the supervision of contracts with utilities and private actors, monitor utilities' financing activities, increase public participation, offer consumer protection (including dispute resolution) and address water sector challenges through capacity building.

The five countries in the region may need to address tariffs (which are too low to cover operation and maintenance) (Table 0.2), as well as lack of data, law enforcement, monitoring of services performance and limited human resource capacity. Complex challenges such as governance and financial sustainability are found across the Mekong region with respect to accessing water infrastructure. Addressing these challenges will be critical.

Table 0.2. Water and wastewater regulation challenges in Mekong countries

Country	Key regulatory challenges
Cambodia	Low tariffs; weak policy enforcement, particularly in rural areas; infrequent data collection; and different definitions of terms among jurisdictions
Lao PDR	Low tariffs; weak monitoring; reports written in Lao language hinder external analysis
Myanmar	Lack of co-ordination among multiple agencies in wastewater treatment regulation; lack of, or inaccessible, data
Thailand	Low tariffs; weak enforcement of regulation
Viet Nam	Low tariffs; weak monitoring of service delivery and shortage of human capital

Cambodia

The urban-rural gap is one of the major challenges in water infrastructure in Cambodia. Water systems in rural areas lag behind those of Phnom Penh. Nearly all residents of Phnom Penh have drinking water piped into their dwellings. Elsewhere, less than 60% of residents have piped water. Differences in definitions of terms and policies among jurisdictions have contributed to the gap in drinking water access. Standardising the definitions is therefore essential to improve access. Shortage of physical and human capital, weak law enforcement and credibility of institutions also remain challenging.

Lao PDR

Water conservation is one of the key barriers in Lao PDR. The country does not promote demand management or provide incentives for research and development of conservation technologies. Monitoring of service performance also needs to improve. The reporting structure of water quality is robust. However, reports are written in Lao and highly inaccessible, making it difficult for an external analysis of water quality to be carried out. Responsibilities for funding are delegated to the Water Supply Development Fund, but much of the funding is external. Tax and fee breaks on investment and operation encourage involvement, but poor revenue collection, along with high operating costs, discourage external investment.

Myanmar

In Myanmar, the development and enforcement of quality standards for drinking water are challenges that must be addressed. Efforts are needed to improve institutional efficiency and ensure sufficient infrastructure for wastewater treatment in urban areas. Multiple agencies are involved in wastewater treatment regulation, and inter-agency co-ordination needs improvement. There is also room for further conservation efforts. State-owned irrigation systems do not recover costs, making maintenance or upgrades difficult.

Thailand

Thailand appears to have appropriate water regulation given its legislative challenges. Improvement will be needed in the enforcement of legislation and the development of foreign investment opportunities in the Thai water sector. Water contamination is common due to regulations being ignored. Environmental impact studies of construction projects are only undertaken upon request, putting water supplies at further risk of contamination. Low water tariffs are also a challenge as they have remained mostly unchanged since the 1940s and are far below the amount required to cover operational costs.

Viet Nam

Viet Nam possesses robust water regulations in general. However, more efforts are needed to enforce regulation, monitor service delivery and develop human capital. Licensing and quality standards are in place for wastewater treatment, but most wastewater flows into streams untreated, harming downstream water quality. Water conservation policies exist, but enforcement is far from straightforward, contributing to weak compliance. In addition, as with every other Mekong country for which tariff data are available, tariff schedules struggle to cover operation and maintenance costs.

References

OECD (2020), *Economic Outlook for Southeast Asia, China and India 2020 – Update: Meeting the Challenges of COVID-19*, OECD Publishing, Paris, https://dx.doi.org/10.1787/e8c90b68-en. [2]

OECD (2018), *Road and Rail Infrastructure in Asia: Investing in Quality*, The Development Dimension, OECD Publishing, Paris, https://dx.doi.org/10.1787/9789264302563-en. [1]

WHO-UNICEF (2020), *Joint Monitoring Programme for Water Supply, Sanitation and Hygiene (database)*, https://sdg6data.org/tables (accessed on 13 May 2020). [3]

1 Key water-related development challenges in the Mekong River Basin – Brief overview

This chapter provides an overview of the socio-economic and environmental challenges concerning the Mekong River. It also discusses the initiatives towards further regional co-operation, with a focus on mutual efforts to enhance climate resilience. The chapter also reviews the economic benefits of the Mekong River in terms of agriculture and fisheries, navigation and trade, tourism, hydropower, water supply and sediment extraction. The likely impact of climate change on wetlands, biodiversity and aquaculture is subsequently addressed. The chapter concludes with a discussion about the need to build on transboundary co-operation efforts to preserve both the economic gains and ecosystem services that benefit millions of people in the Mekong River Basin.

Introduction

Countries in the Mekong River Basin (MRB) have recorded impressive economic growth, mainly due to the opportunities provided by the Mekong River. The river serves as a lifeline to millions who dwell in the MRB, providing irrigation (for agriculture), work and revenue in fisheries and sediment extraction, water supply, hydropower, and opportunities for tourism.

Any large-scale development of the river must consider that riparian communities may have different priorities for river use such as hydropower (Lao People's Democratic Republic, hereafter "Lao PDR"); water in agriculture (Thailand and Viet Nam); and fisheries (Cambodia). In addition, the People's Republic of China (hereafter "China"), Lao PDR, Thailand and Viet Nam use the navigable course of the river as a trade route (WWF-Greater Mekong, 2016[1]).

Furthermore, climate modelling based on the downscaled climate change data sets (AR5 - 2014 of the Intergovernmental Panel on Climate Change – IPCC) applied by the Mekong River Commission (MRC) under its Climate Change Adaptation Initiative (CCAI) showed that the MRB is among the river basins most vulnerable to climate change (Oeurng et al., 2019[2]). Adaptation to climate change for riparian communities in transboundary river basins calls for increased co-operation in terms of regional security and economic development.

To bolster co-operation, the Asian Development Bank and six countries of the Greater Mekong Subregion (GMS) launched the *GMS Economic Cooperation Program* to enhance economic relations in 1992; the MRC was established in 1995; the *Ayeyawady–Chao Phraya–Mekong Economic Co-operation Strategy* engaged Cambodia, Lao PDR, Myanmar, Thailand and Viet Nam to promote development in the sub-region in 2003; in 2015, China launched the *Lancang-Mekong Cooperation (LMC)*, which identified five areas of necessary policy action: agriculture and rural development, cross-border economic co-operation, production capacity, connectivity, and water resources. These initiatives provide a strong foundation for further transboundary co-operation on MRB issues.

Key water-related development challenges in the Mekong River

The Mekong River originates approximately 5 200 metres above sea level at the Tibetan Plateau and discharges into the South China Sea after travelling 4 350 kilometres. The river drains a 795 000 km^2 catchment area, and has the eighth-largest annual discharge volume (475 km^3) in the world (MRC, 2010[3]). The Mekong Delta is characterised by a wide riverbed and numerous estuaries. The characteristics of the river and the delta make their influence on socio-economic development large, particularly, in Thailand, Cambodia, Lao PDR and Viet Nam. The MRB is host to some of the richest biodiversity in the world, and species of animals and plants continue to be discovered. The Mekong holds three times more fish species per unit area than the Amazon River (WWF, n.d.[4]). 115 species of plants and animals were discovered in MRB countries in 2016 and an even greater number were discovered the following year. (WWF, 2017[5]). The MRB wetlands are also important biodiversity hotspots that play an important role in the economy, society and culture of the region (WWF-Greater Mekong, 2016[1]).

This chapter discusses the following key socio-economic and environmental challenges facing the Mekong River:

- irrigation, sanitation and water supply quality
- water transportation infrastructure
- hydropower development
- climate change response
- tourism.

Irrigation is the primary use of water in the Mekong River Basin

Irrigation is the major beneficiary of the Mekong River, using 70% of its water resources. The total irrigated area in the basin is approximately four million hectares, and irrigated areas are expanding steadily in many countries. Sixty per cent of the MRB population is engaged in agriculture. However, the majority are smallholder farmers who cultivate less than two hectares, and depend mostly on household members for labour (MRC, 2018[6]), thus limiting the GDP contribution of the sector to about 14% (MRC, 2018[7]). The relatively fertile flood plain, riverine and deltaic areas have higher population densities. These areas host most of the major urban population centres in the basin, including Phnom Penh, Vientiane, Udon Thani and Ubon Ratchaathani and Can Tho. North-eastern Thailand and Viet Nam's Mekong Delta account for most of the irrigation (by area) in the Mekong region (Table 1.1). Expansion of agriculture in the basin is limited by water availability in the dry season.

Table 1.1. Irrigated area of the MRB by country

Country	Percentage of irrigated area in MRB
Cambodia	8
Lao PDR	7
Myanmar	2
Thailand	30
Viet Nam	42
China	12

Source: (FAO, 2016[8]), *AQUASTAT* website, http://www.fao.org/nr/water/aquastat/countries_regions/profile_segments/mekong-IrrDr_eng.stm.

Reservoir dams upstream may be able to support the storage of water during the dry season, providing a boost to the agricultural sector. In the next 20 years, there are plans to increase dry season irrigated area by 50% (from 1.2 to 1.8 million hectares). Lao PDR is planning to expand irrigated area from less than 100 000 hectares to more than 300 000 hectares (MRC, 2018[7]). Cambodia is also considering a major expansion of its irrigated area (Lacombe and McCartney, 2016[9]). The construction of reservoirs and dams along the Mekong River and its tributaries has altered the migration pattern of fish in some areas. Sanitation and water supply quality need improvement.

The pressure exerted by population growth and socio-economic development has posed considerable challenges for communities to access safe water. Between 2018 and 2060, the basin's population is projected to rise from about 65 million to about 83 million. Rapid industrialisation and urbanisation lead to reduced land for agriculture, increased demand for clean water and more wastewater. These demands place an enormous burden on the Mekong's water resources (MRC, 2016[10]).

Throughout the Mekong River region, research on water quality has focused on large bodies of water such as the main river canals. Pollutants and contaminants are often diluted in those areas due to the enormous volumes of water. However, other studies show that local communities primarily use large river sources for irrigation or navigation while using smaller tributaries and canals near their homes for daily water supply, hygiene and sanitation needs. Unfortunately, these smaller water sources have much higher concentrations of pollutants and contaminants (Sebesvari and Renaud, 2017[11]). Research on how to preserve the quality of these vital drinking water supplies is currently lacking.

Cambodia and Lao PDR are the MRB countries with the least access to proper sanitation and piped or connected water supply services. Studies suggest that untreated sewage makes up a major portion of water pollution in canals and smaller tributaries of the Mekong River, especially those in densely populated areas (Chea, Grenouillet and Lek, 2016[12]). Limited availability of water, sanitation and hygiene facilities, as well as inadequate behaviour, are major contributors to the high rate of waterborne and foodborne diseases in MRB countries (Smajgl and Ward, 2013[13]).

Mekong River greatly influences water transportation infrastructure development

The Mekong River is the river course for inland and transboundary (international) water transport. The upstream section of the river is suitable for inland navigation from river ports in Yunnan, China, running to Lao PDR and then reaching Kompong Channang in Cambodia. The downstream section of the river is navigable by both inland and maritime transport (MRC, 2018[7]). Trade along the river generates economic benefits, but increased traffic can pose environmental risks to the river and safety risks to its users. The MRC's Navigation Programme is designed to address these concerns by establishing legal principles with respect to navigation and increasing international trade opportunities for MRC member countries, while ensuring safe and effective river transportation (MRC, 2012[14]).

Unlike the Mekong River, the Mekong Delta can accommodate larger vessels in greater numbers. It handles 78% of the annual cargo volume, and 89% of the passenger traffic on the Mekong. The upper stretch of the river between China and Cambodia is only navigable by smaller vessels carrying less than 250 tonnes. The middle stretches from Thailand to Cambodia via Lao PDR can accommodate larger vessels carrying more than 300 tonnes (UNECE, 2019[15]).

Although the delta has more than 30 000 kilometres of rivers and canals, port infrastructure usually operates below capacity. The lack of connectivity between the inland waterways, ports and road networks severely limits efficiency. There are 7 seaports, 31 harbours and 57 inland ports in the Mekong Delta. In spite of this, around 80% of goods are still transported by land to seaports in the region (Dezan Shira and Associates, 2018[16]). Development of connectivity may further enhance the region's economic potential.

The development of inland waterways transport (IWT) in the upper reaches of the Mekong (above the Khone Falls) is constrained by narrow and turbulent sections of the river and large seasonal variations in water levels. The Mekong River does provide an important link in the transit route between Kunming, China and Bangkok, Thailand. An estimated 800 000 tonnes of IWT cargo are shipped annually among China, Thailand, Myanmar and Lao PDR (MRC, 2018[7]).

IWT trade in the Lower Mekong River has grown in recent years, with a steady increase in container traffic at Phnom Penh Port and in general cargo through Can Tho Port. IWT trade received a significant boost with the opening of a new deep-water port at Cai Mep in Viet Nam, where terminals accommodate some of the largest container ships in the world. Cargo can therefore be shipped internationally to and from Phnom Penh with a single trans-shipment at Cai Mep (MRC, 2009[17]).

Recent estimates suggested that IWT cargo volumes increased from approximately 15 million tonnes in 2007 to 23 million tonnes in 2014, an average annual growth rate of 6.4% (MRC, 2017[18]). The annual net economic value of cargo transportation in 2007 was estimated at USD 6.8 billion. Viet Nam had the largest share at USD 5.1 billion, followed by Cambodia (USD 1.1 billion), Lao PDR (USD 0.4 billion) and Thailand (USD 0.2 billion) (MRC, 2017[18]). Viet Nam's waterways carry a much higher proportion of the national freight (almost 19% in terms of tonne-kilometres) compared to the other leading IWT regions (for instance, China, the United States and the European Union carry 5-8% each). Globally, the volume of freight carried by waterways increased from 73 million tonnes in 2014 to 80 million tonnes in 2015, an increase of 8.8% year-on-year.

The number of passengers travelling on IWT transport (i.e. speed boats and cruise vessels) in the Mekong River is significant. An estimated 63 000 passengers, including tourists, are transported annually in Cambodia and Viet Nam (MRC, 2017[18]). To continue spurring growth in both of these areas, MRB countries need to invest in increasing the port capacity and expanding the network to increase connectivity and efficiency (MRC, 2017[18]).

Hydropower represents a source of growth despite infrastructure and environmental concerns

MRB hydropower sources are important for all MRB countries, supplying 10% of electricity demand. Lao PDR derives nearly all of its supply from MRB hydropower, while Cambodia obtains more than one-third of its electricity supply from hydropower plants in the basin. Thailand has the lowest share of MRB hydropower in its supply mix, including significant hydropower imports from Lao PDR. Viet Nam covers around 9% of its demand from plants in the central highlands (MRC, 2018[7]). The MRC believes hydropower would create great economic and energy gains. However, it also raises concerns about the potential impacts of infrastructure and operation on the environment, fisheries and the livelihoods of people in the MRB.

The river structure and flow make it highly suitable for hydropower generation, especially near the border between China and Lao PDR where elevation of the river drops by 400 metres in a short distance (MRC, 2018[19]). Countries seeking to reduce their dependence on fossil fuels are transitioning to more renewable energy sources. Hydropower is the only clean energy source that can fuel rapid economic growth in MRB countries. Hundreds of hydropower projects and dams (regulating, storage, etc.) along the Mekong are at various stages of development from planning to completion (Figure 1.1). The above figure excludes projects in the Mekong tributaries. It is estimated that large-scale hydropower dams could generate 30 000 megawatts of electricity for the region. To fulfil this potential, regional governments are taking into account the construction of 88 additional dams in the Lower Mekong River basin by 2030 (Sassoon, 2017[20]).

Figure 1.1. Overview of existing and planned hydropower projects in the MRB

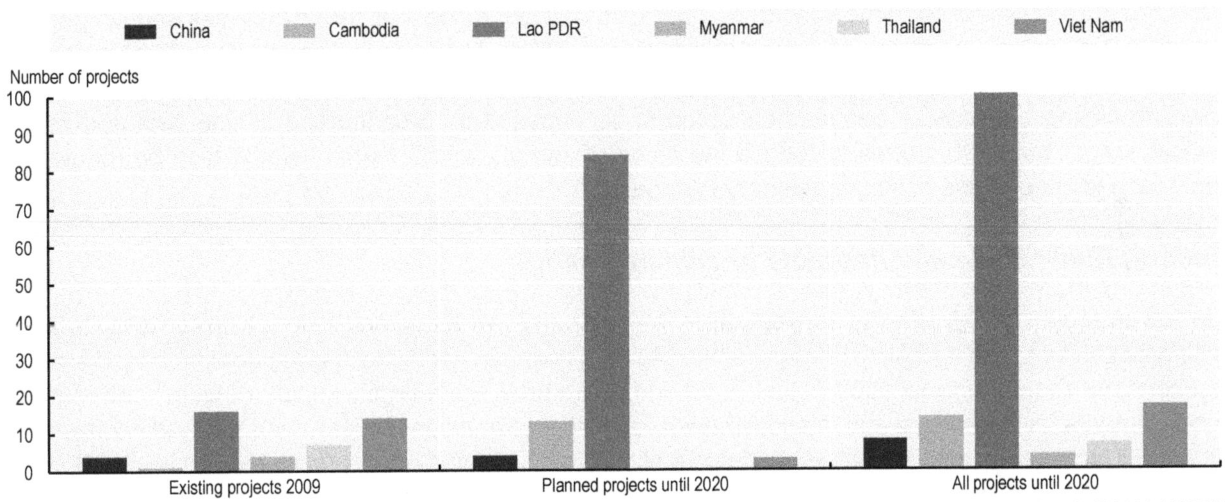

StatLink https://doi.org/10.1787/888934167581

Source: (Vu and Mayer, 2018[21]; Kuenzer et al., 2012[22]).

Furthermore, more than 120 dams are planned for Mekong tributaries and 11 large-scale hydropower dams are slated for the Mekong mainstream, which could produce more than 13 000 megawatts (MW) of hydropower. While Thailand and Viet Nam have already developed most of their tributary sites, Cambodia, Lao PDR and Myanmar possess the greatest potential for hydropower resource development (Open Development Mekong, 2017[23]). By 2030, these three countries are expected to generate 96% of their power through hydroelectricity (ICEM, 2010[24]).

Excess hydropower can also be exported to neighbouring countries. Only about 10% of the hydroelectricity generated in Cambodia and Lao PDR will remain in-country, while the rest is intended for export (Open Development Mekong, 2017[23]). Lao PDR, which aims to be the "Battery of Asia", intends to export electricity to its neighbours and other member states of the Association of Southeast Asian Nations (ASEAN). National banks and multinational companies from China, Thailand and Viet Nam have formed private-public partnerships with host governments of the MRB to build hydroelectric dams in the region.

Hydropower could contribute to the reduction of greenhouse gas emissions, yet as climate change alters water availability, changing rainfall patterns could reduce or alter the flow of rivers, threatening the potential of hydropower. For example, between 2014 and 2017, an unprecedented drought reduced water pressure in hydroelectric plants in Brazil, resulting in increased water consumption tariffs (UNFCCC, 2018[25]). Most climate scenarios predict more extreme dry periods, thus calling for alternative sources of power such as solar to be explored (MRC, 2018[26]).

Development of hydropower projects along the Lancang-Mekong necessitates the regular assessment of hydropower's impact on sedimentation, river flow and level fluctuations and fishery needs. MRB countries still have large rural populations that are predominantly employed in agriculture and fisheries. Proper fishery management is therefore essential to ensure the survival of fishing-related industries. In Lao PDR, the value of the fisheries is equivalent to nearly 13% of the country's GDP. Although proportionally less significant to the national economy, the Mekong fisheries in Thailand and Viet Nam add well over USD 5.5 billion to their GDP annually (MRC, 2015[27]).

Mekong countries have made efforts to protect fishery resources. In 2010, Cambodia and Lao PDR signed a memorandum of understanding on fishery management and strategies for transboundary fishing. In 2015, China and Lao PDR signed a co-operation agreement to protect fishery resources. The agreement delineates 40 kilometres of the river from the Chinese and Lao PDR border as a common protected area. It creates a framework for co-operation that clearly defines responsibilities and obligations, including joint enforcement and releasing of fish stocks (MRC, 2017[28]). In August 2017, the Cambodian government announced that the provincial departments of agriculture would be given more powers to crack down on fishing offences. A ban was expected to be imposed on 3-centimetre fishing nets and fishing devices longer than 300 metres to reduce the catch of immature fish. Fishers would also be required to apply for a licence to use fishing machinery (Vannak, 2017[29]).

Mekong River Basin is vulnerable to climate change

Several emerging issues affect water security in the Mekong River Basin and its inhabitants' ability to adapt to climate change. The hydrological cycle of the Mekong is driven mainly by the regional monsoon climate, resulting in a regular annual flood pulse. The flood pulse provides a timely supply of water and nutrient-rich sediments for agriculture and inland fisheries, as well as extensive instream and wetland ecosystems. As such, it represents an essential driving force for life, livelihoods and major ecosystems in the MRB (Arias et al., 2013[30]). The livelihoods of a growing number of people living in the basin (approximately 65 million currently) are intertwined with the health of the river (MRC, 2018[7]), however, the future of the hydrological cycle of the Mekong is in question as a result of climate uncertainties. Climate modelling shows that the MRB will experience changes in flow and alteration in its annual flood cycle. The river's original structure and hydrological cycle may be altered as a result of increasing use and demand for raw water, food and energy in the region. Land use and other human activities further compound the effects of climate change.

Weather pattern changes affect the agriculture production cycle and fish breeding. Changes in water level and flow affect navigation routes and operation of hydropower plants and reservoirs. Sediment flow is also altered due to changes in flood pulse. Large water storage structures and extraction for irrigation further compound alterations to sediment flow. A 2009 Mekong River Delta Climate Change Forum Report showed that saline intrusion has reached further inland affecting large areas of the Delta region. Saline intrusion is a typically-occurring phenomenon owing to seasonal discharge fluctuations, however it has been exacerbated recently by rising sea levels, and abnormally low water volumes. If the intrusion expands into the agricultural area of the Delta, it will cause further decline in agricultural productivity of the region (CGIAR Research Program on CCAFS SEA, 2016[31]). Furthermore, increased vulnerability to floods and drought in the basin will affect livelihoods and undermine agricultural productivity. The wet season is also projected to shorten slightly and the corresponding extension of the dry season suggests greater likelihood of drought periods when combined with warmer temperatures. Studies about future climate impacts in the Mekong Basin broadly share a set of common themes: increased temperature and annual precipitation, increased flood intensities in the Mekong Delta and Cambodian floodplain, variability in runoff, prolonged droughts in the south and east of the basin, and sea-level rise and salinity intrusion in the Mekong Delta (Evers and Pathirana, 2018[32]). The Mekong River Basin is vulnerable to several climate change impacts that include a predicted mean temperature rise of approximately 0.8°C by 2030. A regional increase in annual precipitation of 200 millimetres is also anticipated (MRC, 2018[7]).

The dry season brings unpredictable fairway conditions to the upper and middle portions of the Mekong River, rendering navigation difficult and unsafe. Extended periods of drought exacerbate this problem. Moreover, navigability of the river in the MRB is further threatened by sand mining. Few larger river ports are available on the upper stretch and most of the trans-shipment is done directly via the natural riverbank (Mekong Institute, 2016[33]).

MRC basin-wide assessments of climate impact on flood behaviour suggest that flooded areas might increase by 2060. At Chiang Saen, annual sediment flows have decreased from about 85 megatonnes (Mt) to 10.8 Mt. This indicates a reduction in sediments from China to the Mekong mainstream from 55% to about 16%. A similar trend is seen downstream at Pakse, where average annual loads decreased from 147 Mt to 66 Mt between 1994 and 2013. Changes in sediment concentrations, brought about by the construction of storage reservoirs, signal a substantial and seemingly permanent change in the river's morphology (MRC, 2018[7]).

Even at present, floods continue to damage the economies of MRC member countries. Data for the five years between 2010-14 show the annual cost of flood damage varied between USD 20 million in 2012 and USD 500 million in 2011. The average cost was USD 200 million per year (MRC, 2018[34]). The rising of the sea level is threatening the region's coastal communities, adding stress to coastal ecosystems such as mangroves. These have already suffered due to large-scale conversion for rice cultivation and aquaculture of shrimp and fish. By the end of the century, higher sea levels in the Mekong Delta, where nearly half of Viet Nam's rice is grown, may inundate half of the delta's agricultural lands (approximately 1.4 million hectares) and displace millions of people (WWF, 2009[35]).

The rapidly-growing aquaculture sector (2.1 Mt in 2012, compared with 0.7 Mt in 2002) compensates for the decline in capture fisheries, but creates pollution and destroys wetlands due to unsustainable management and operational practices (MRC, 2018[7]). Fishing effort has increased to cope with growing demand, and smaller fish currently make up an increasing proportion of the total catch. However, the growth is necessary to cover the shortage brought on by increased urbanisation, changing consumption patterns and growing export markets. Thus, aquaculture is increasingly important to the basin's economy and food security. Viet Nam is the leader in this area, accounting for 86% of Mekong countries' aquaculture production.

Sediment extraction exceeds rate of replacement and stresses ecosystems

The Mekong River serves other vital functions in its riparian ecosystems, such as sediment transport. Sediments serve as a major carrier and storage agent for nutrients such as phosphorus, nitrogen and potassium. Sediment carriage by the river is the main contributor to the immense productivity of the Tonle Sap River and the Mekong Delta (WWF-Greater Mekong, 2016[11]). The deposited sediment preserves the shape of riverbeds and deltas, contributes to crop and fishery productivity, provides construction and land reclamation material, and creates habitable and cultivable landscapes (WWF-Greater Mekong, 2016[11]).

The lake retains about 80% of the sediment and nutrients carried into it by the flow reversal. This has been the main factor underpinning the success of wet rice cultivation and fisheries in Cambodia. Many Mekong River fish species are migratory, crossing national boundaries during their lifecycle driven by hydrological pulses (Neiland and Béné, 2008[36]). Fishing and related activities are the primary economic activity for nearly 80% of the labour force in Cambodia and the fishery depends directly on seasonal flooding of the lake (Seng, 2019[37]).

Studies found that more than 55 million tonnes of sediment were extracted from the Mekong main stem in Lao PDR, Thailand, Cambodia and Viet Nam in 2011. This is a conservative estimate as it covers neither the tributaries nor the upper Mekong (WWF-Greater Mekong, 2018[38]). Dam reservoirs trap part of the suspended load of sediment (silt, clay and fine sand) and most of the bed load (sand and gravel), reducing the sediment load in the river downstream. Dams are thought to have already reduced the volume of sediment from 160 Mt before 1994 to 75 Mt in 2014. One study modelled a future reduction of sediment flow in the delta of 51%, based on 38 existing and planned dams (WWF-Greater Mekong, 2018[38]). Sediment extraction is a problem in Cambodia (60% of extraction volume in 2011-12), Viet Nam, Thailand and Lao PDR. In 2009, Cambodia banned the export of sand following concerns over the volumes exported to Singapore for land reclamation and Viet Nam followed suit the same year. However, local sand consumption remains high in these two countries due to economic growth that fuels construction (WWF-Greater Mekong, 2018[38]), even though studies have shown that natural sediment supplies from the upper reaches of the Mekong are insufficient to compensate for the loss of extracted bed aggregates. This shows the non-sustainable nature of local sand mining (Jordan et al., 2019[39]).

Mekong River's tourism potential remains relatively untapped

Water is an important tourism resource, which could significantly influence the attractiveness of a destination. Water-based tourism can take several forms depending on the characteristics of the body of water upon which it is reliant. As such, a broad distinction can be made between maritime tourism, on one hand, and river and lake tourism on the other. It is further possible to differentiate between cultural (e.g. heritage sites, landscapes) and leisure and well-being activities (e.g. sailing, diving, balneotherapy).

The MRB region is one of the leading tourist arrival regions in the world, with about 60 million international arrivals in 2017 (Mekong Tourism Coordinating Office). In 2017, the Mekong Delta received over 22.4 million tourists, generating USD 495 million in revenue. In 2016, Can Tho and Kien Giang were the two most-visited places in the delta. Tourism income for the two destinations reached USD 127.6 million and USD 201.4 million, respectively (Dezan Shira and Associates, 2018[16]). Delta tourism potential lies in areas such as ecotourism, resorts and exploration tourism. The tourism industry could create an additional 300 000 jobs in the delta by 2025, leading to a sustainable and diversified regional economy (Dezan Shira and Associates, 2018[16]). Furthermore, Viet Nam's delta region is the most heavily cruised segment of the Mekong. Its main attractions include floating markets and villages, its maze of canals, cultural and historical sites, community-based tourism and distinct natural environment. The delta's popularity is also due to its proximity to, and ease of access from, Ho Chi Minh City – an international air hub and first-tier destination (UNWTO, 2016[40]).

In Cambodia, the UNESCO World Heritage site of Angkor is a well-recognised attraction in the region. It is not located on the Mekong River, but linked by a 100-kilometre channel and the Tonle Sap Lake (UNWTO, 2016[40]). River tourism is growing steadily in Cambodia, although many opportunities exist for further development. Phnom Penh plays a pivotal role, as it is the geographical hub for cruises to and from the Mekong Delta, Tonle Sap Lake, Siem Reap and the Mekong Discovery Trail running to the Lao PDR border. However, the Trail is under-used due to lack of promotion and poor cross-border connectivity (UNWTO, 2016[40]).

The Mekong River Valley characterises the landscape of the western boundary of Lao PDR and the Mekong flows through areas of Lao PDR otherwise inaccessible. The sights and adventures of river travel in this area are unique and a tourism resource of significant potential for the country (UNWTO, 2016[40]). More of the Mekong River lies in Lao PDR than in all other MRB countries combined, yet its river-based tourism potential remains relatively untapped. The well-established Luang Prabang to HoueiXay route and cruise activities in southern Champassak province reflect the potential of Mekong tourism. Currently, Lao PDR and Thai government officials are focusing on the possible development of a Luang Prabang–Chiang Saen route (UNWTO, 2016[40]).

The Mekong dominates Thailand's lengthy northern and north-eastern borders. However, cruise tourism and river-based activities play a minor role compared to Cambodia, Lao PDR and Viet Nam. The Tourism Authority of Thailand has had limited success in promoting river destinations in the northeast of the country (UNWTO, 2016[40]). Boat landings tend to be well developed at locations most frequented by overland tourists and cargo vessels such as Cambodia's capital Phnom Penh and Chiang Saen, Thailand. Construction of modern piers, such as the ones in My Tho in Viet Nam, and Chiang Khan in Thailand, have driven river-based tourism. Other key Mekong destinations, including Luang Prabang and Vientiane in Lao PDR, could benefit from major improvements to boating infrastructure. Various opportunities to develop new types of river-based tourism products (e.g. adventure tourism) along the Mekong River and its tributaries are relatively unexplored due to a general lack of awareness of river-based tourism development (UNWTO, 2016[40]).

Transboundary co-operation is essential for climate adaptation

Due to the transboundary nature of the river and socio-economic impact of climate change, MRB countries need to strengthen co-operation to implement basin-wide climate adaptation measures (Table 1.2). MRB countries must come together to establish mutual understanding of the impact of climate change on the Mekong River and its ability to support socio-economic growth. Subsequently, they should implement basin-wide climate adaptation programmes and measures. The absence of such measures could erode the substantial economic gains of MRB countries by affecting the livelihoods and lives of their citizens.

Co-operation enables joint development of more cost-effective solutions, which potentially offer benefits to riparian parties. For example, exchanging information and combining impact assessments and model results throughout the basin can increase the reliability of modelling results. Transboundary co-operation in adaptation also helps deploy such measures as flood protection infrastructure where they can have the optimal effect. Costs and benefits of adaptation are shared and increase the overall efficiency and effectiveness of adaptation in the basin (UNECE and INBO, 2015[41]).

Water is the main theme for transboundary co-operation in the Mekong. Following recognition of the need for transboundary and shared governance of the river basin early in the 1950s, the United Nations helped establish the Mekong River Committee, which became the Mekong River Commission in 1995. Four of the six Mekong countries are full-time members of the Commission, while China and Myanmar hold observer status. Table 1.2 on the following page presents a summary of examples of transboundary water governance initiatives since 1992.

Table 1.2. Transboundary water governance (examples)

Year	Transboundary co-operation mechanism of Mekong River	Members	Description
1992	Greater Mekong Subregion	Cambodia, Lao PDR, Myanmar, Thailand and Viet Nam, and Yunnan and GuangXi province of China	ADB and other donors supported the Greater Mekong Subregion (GMS) program to implement high-priority sub-regional projects in agriculture, energy, environment, health and human resource development, information and communication technology, tourism, transport and trade facilitation and urban development.
1995	Mekong River Commission (MRC)	Cambodia, Lao PDR, Thailand and Viet Nam	Previously known as the Mekong Committee, the MRC is the inter-governmental organisation that works directly with the governments to jointly manage the shared water resources and the sustainable development of the Mekong River.
1996	ASEAN-Mekong Basin Development Cooperation	ASEAN-MRB countries and China	Promotes economic integration among the member countries. Contributes to the development of infrastructure and human capital in the sub-region and enables the sharing of the resource between ASEAN Member States, Mekong riparian countries, and China.
2000	Mekong-Ganga Cooperation Program	Cambodia, Lao PDR, Myanmar, Thailand, Viet Nam and India	Co-operation in tourism, culture, education, as well as transport and communications.
2000	Joint Committee on Coordination of Commercial Navigation on the Lancang-Mekong River	China, Lao PDR, Myanmar and Thailand	Co-ordinates implementation of the agreement on commercial navigation on the Lancang-Mekong River
2003	Ayeyarawady/Irrawady-Chao Phraya–Mekong Economic Cooperation Strategy	Cambodia, Lao PDR, Myanmar, Thailand and Viet Nam	Economic co-operation using self-help and partnership to achieve sustainable development, including poverty reduction.
2009	Lower Mekong Initiative	Cambodia, Lao PDR, Myanmar, Thailand and Viet Nam, initiated by the United States	Serves as a platform to address complex, transnational development and policy challenges in the Lower Mekong sub-region under six pillars: 1. Environment and Water (co-chaired by Viet Nam and the United States) 2. Health (co-chaired by Cambodia and the United States) 3. Agriculture (co-chaired by Myanmar and the United States) 4. Connectivity (co-chaired by Lao PDR and the United States) 5. Education (co-chaired by Thailand and the United States) 6. Energy Security (co-chaired by Thailand and the United States)
2015	Lancang-Mekong Cooperation	China, Cambodia, Lao PDR, Myanmar, Thailand, Viet Nam	China led co-operation in five areas: 1. Production capacity 2. Water resources 3. Connectivity 4. Agriculture and poverty reduction 5. Cross-border economic co-operation.

Source: Authors.

Australian Aid, the International Water Management Institute, the Institut de Recherche pour le Développement and Chiang Mai University collaborated to analyse transboundary water governance in the Lower Mekong region. The study highlighted the diversity of actors and the role of decision tools in water resource allocation (Dore, Lebel and Molle, 2012[42]). Co-operation has been established in the MRB since the middle of the 20th century to foster increased regional connectivity through different goals, targets and priority areas (Xu, Bao and Zhou, 2006[43]). These initiatives are described in the following sub-sections.

Regional bilateralism is an important building block for climate resilience

Economic and energy-related development and security factors across the Mekong region have resulted in a trend of "regional bilateralism". In this approach, key decisions and investment deals regarding transboundary water resource developments are largely made outside of international frameworks. Instead, they remain cross-border measures between the strongest economies in the region (Thailand and Viet Nam) or among the less industrialised, but resource-rich countries (Cambodia, Lao PDR and Myanmar) (Open Development Mekong, 2017[23]).

In the context of a transboundary climate change adaptation strategy, the MRC has drafted the Mekong Adaptation Strategy and Action Plan (MASAP). This considers MRC's 2016-2020 Integrated Water Resources Management-based Basin Development Strategy, the 2016-2020 Strategic Plan, and the 2009-2025 Climate Change and Adaptation Initiative Framework Document. The MASAP focuses on seven priority areas: the mainstreaming of climate change adaptation into national policies; co-operation and partnership; a transboundary and gender-sensitive adaptation framework; adaptation finance; monitoring, data collection and sharing; capacity building; and communication and outreach (MRC, 2018[44]).

MRC also engages external partners such as ASEAN, the Lancang-Mekong Cooperation, donors, international financial institutions and other climate change stakeholders. The presence of regional policies and a vision to adopt technological solutions for climate change adaptation provide a strong foundation for regional climate-resilience building processes (Sembiring, 2018[45]).

Navigation and trade benefitted from joint initiatives in the region

In 2009, the MRC's Navigation Programme facilitated the Agreement on Waterway Transport between Cambodia and Viet Nam. Through the programme, the MRC and China expressed a commitment to improve navigation safety on the Lancang-Mekong River. Myanmar is also included to improve navigation on the Upper and Lower Mekong River (MRC, 2012[14]).

Navigation programmes have helped increase trade in the region. Trade volume between Southwest China's Yunnan Province and the five countries along the Mekong River grew by 13.4% year-on-year in the provincial capital of Kunming, reaching USD 12 billion in 2017, according to data provided by the customs authorities. Customs authorities in Kunming and Mekong River countries co-operated by exchanging information, fighting cross-border crime and working together on customs clearing (XinhuaNet, 2019[46]).

China, Myanmar, Lao PDR and Thailand conducted 73 joint patrols on some areas along the Lancang-Mekong River from December 2011 to late August 2018, especially in the dangerous Golden Triangle area. These aimed to crack down on transnational crimes; protect the security of the ships, goods and people on the river; and ensure that this vital waterway is safe and flourishing (XinhuaNet, 2018[47]).

China has implemented programmes for dredging and provided navigation aids for the first 331 kilometres along the river from Yunnan to Lao PDR. This is expected to allow navigational passage for 100-150 deadweight tonnage vessels for at least 95% of the year, enhancing cross-border water transport, trade facilitation and safety, which also helps growth in the tourism sector (Mekong Institute, 2016[33]). The Joint Committee on Coordination of Commercial Navigation was established in 2002 by China, Lao PDR, Myanmar and Thailand to improve safe navigation on the Mekong (and Lancang) River. Member countries need to review their agreement on commercial navigation on the Lancang-Mekong River. The agreement must be updated to reflect the imminent threat from climate change and recent developments in the Mekong, which have bearing on the safe navigation of the river.

Full co-operation appears more difficult than bilateral and multilateral co-operation when it comes to economic conditions in the river basin. Each partner has adopted different preferences for co-operation targets. Co-operation with more defined objectives was easier to establish than with broader and more complex objectives (Feng et al., 2019[48]).

Several initiatives towards shared water resources management are underway

Water resources co-operation is one of the five priority areas of the LMC and is also the flagship field that members seem to value the most. Through the Sanya Declaration, leaders agreed to enhance co-operation among LMC countries in sustainable management and use of water resources. They also pledged more co-operation through technical exchanges, capacity building, drought and flood mitigation, data and information sharing, as well as joint research and analysis related to resources of the Lancang-Mekong River Basin (Embassy of the P.R. China in Thailand, 2019[49]). The LMC's Joint Working Group on Water Resources recently established the following thematic areas for action on water resources:

- sustainable hydropower development and energy security
- integrated water resources management and climate change adaptation
- transboundary river co-operation and information sharing
- water resources and green development
- rural areas water conservancy and livelihood improvement
- water sector production capacity co-operation.

The LMC secretariat and its members should monitor and evaluate the impact of these with respect to the Sustainable Development Goals. Ultimately, the region's development path should not perpetuate environmental and physical degradation of the Mekong River and its tributaries, while mainstreaming climate change adaptation in every area of co-operation.

The Asian Development Bank (ADB) established the GMS Economic Cooperation Program with two provinces of China (Yunnan and Guangxi Zhuang Autonomous Region), Myanmar, Thailand, Lao PDR, Cambodia and Viet Nam. In 2002, the programme's first ten-year strategy was launched. In 2006, due to mounting environmental and climate change concerns, the programme shifted from small projects related to environmental protection to the GMS Core Environment Program (CEP). The first flagship project of GMS-CEP was the Biodiversity Conservation Corridors Initiative. CEP initiatives include: 1) efforts to reduce carbon dioxide emissions in road freight; 2) solutions to build the climate resilience of rural communities; 3) environmental impact assessments; 4) land use modelling; and 5) other tools and approaches for environmentally sustainable economic development. ADB has built partnerships and alliances with MRC to ensure that funds and resources are allocated strategically to avoid duplication of efforts in the region (ADB, 2018[50]).

Competing interests undermine benefits

MRB countries, either through their governments, transboundary co-operation or donor support, have implemented pockets of projects and programmes on their own. These target "climate-smart" agriculture, green freight, food security, sustainable fishery and alternative sources of green energy. However, the benefits of co-operation mechanisms in climate adaptation are not widely realised due to competing economic interests and emphasis on using the Mekong River as a water resource.

Conclusion

The Mekong River plays a significant role in the MRB economies. Socio-economic development in Thailand, Cambodia, Lao PDR and Viet Nam is heavily influenced by the river. It provides irrigation for agriculture, together with opportunities for water transportation and tourism and is a source of hydropower. However, the role and potential of the river cannot be fully maximised, unless the remaining challenges are addressed. Sanitation and water supply quality would need further improvement while climate change and environmental challenges present other concerns. Adaptation to climate change for riparian communities in transboundary river basins calls for increased regional co-operation. A number of initiatives have been implemented among the countries in the region, providing a strong foundation for further transboundary co-operation on MRB-related issues.

References

ADB (2018), *Greater Mekong Subregion Core Environment Program – 10 Years of Cooperation*, Asian Development Bank, Mandaluyong, Manila. [50]

Arias, M. et al. (2013), "The Flood Pulse as the Underlying Driver of Vegetation in the Largest Wetland and Fishery of the Mekong Basin", *AMBIO*, Vol. 42/7, pp. 864-876, http://dx.doi.org/10.1007/s13280-013-0424-4. [30]

CGIAR Research Program on CCAFS SEA (2016), *Assessment Report: The drought and salinity intrusion in the Mekong River Delta of Vietnam*, CGIAR Research Program on Climate Change, Agriculture and Food Security (CCAFS), Hanoi, Viet Nam, https://cgspace.cgiar.org/bitstream/handle/10568/75633/CGIAR%20ASSESSMENT%20REPORT_Mekong_June2.pdf. [31]

Chea, R., G. Grenouillet and S. Lek (2016), "Evidence of Water Quality Degradation in Lower Mekong Basin Revealed by Self-Organizing Map", *PLOS ONE*, Vol. 11/1, http://dx.doi.org/10.1371/journal.pone.0145527. [12]

Dezan Shira and Associates (2018), *"Investment environment in Mekong Delta. Vietnam Briefing"*, Dezan Shira and Associates, https://www.vietnam-briefing.com/news/investment-environment-mekong-delta.html/ (accessed on 13 May 2020). [16]

Dore, J., L. Lebel and F. Molle (2012), "A framework for analysing transboundary water governance complexes, illustrated in the Mekong Region", *Journal of Hydrology*, Vol. 466-467, pp. 23-36, http://dx.doi.org/10.1016/j.jhydrol.2012.07.023. [42]

Embassy of the P.R. China in Thailand (2019), "China and Thailand sign the Memorandum of Understanding on the water resources co-operation on projects of the Lancang-Mekong Cooperation Special Fund", Press Release, 27 December 2009, Bangkok, http://www.chinaembassy.or.th/eng/gdxw/t1728313.htm. [49]

Evers, J. and A. Pathirana (2018), "Adaptation to climate change in the Mekong River Basin: introduction to the special issue", *Climatic Change*, Vol. 149/1, pp. 1-11, http://dx.doi.org/10.1007/s10584-018-2242-y. [32]

FAO (2016), *AQUASTAT website, Food and Agriculture Organisation of the United Nations*, http://www.fao.org/nr/water/aquastat/countries_regions/profile_segments/mekong-IrrDr_eng.stm (accessed on 31 July 2020). [8]

Feng, Y. et al. (2019), "Water Cooperation Priorities in the Lancang-Mekong River Basin Based on Cooperative Events Since the Mekong River Commission Establishment", *Chinese Geographical Science*, Vol. 29/1, pp. 58-69, http://dx.doi.org/10.1007/s11769-019-1016-4. [48]

ICEM (2010), *MRC Strategic Environmental Assessment (SEA) of Hydropower on the Mekong Mainstream*, International Centre for Environmental Management, Mekong River Commission, Vientiane, Hanoi, Viet Nam, https://www.mrcmekong.org/assets/Publications/Consultations/SEA-Hydropower/SEA-Main-Final-Report.pdf. [24]

Jordan, C. et al. (2019), "Sand mining in the Mekong Delta revisited: Current scales of local sediment deficits", *Scientific Reports*, Vol. 9/1, http://dx.doi.org/10.1038/s41598-019-53804-z. [39]

Kuenzer, C. et al. (2012), "Understanding the impact of hydropower developments in the context of upstream–downstream relations in the Mekong river basin", *Sustainability Science*, Vol. 8/4, pp. 565-584, http://dx.doi.org/10.1007/s11625-012-0195-z. [22]

Lacombe, G. and M. McCartney (2016), *Evaluating the flow regulating effects of ecosystems in the Mekong and Volta river basins*, International Water Management Institute (IWMI), http://dx.doi.org/10.5337/2016.202. [9]

Mekong Institute (2016), *Development Potential for International Shipping on the Lancang-Mekong River (China, Lao PDR, Myanmar and Thailand)*, Mekong Institute, Khon Kaen, https://www.mekonginstitute.org/uploads/tx_ffpublication/Development_Potential_for_International_Shipping_on_the_Lancang-Mekong_River__China__Lao_PDR__Myanmar_and_Thailand_.pdf. [33]

MRC (2018), "Basin-Wide Assessment of Climate Change Impacts on Hydropower Production", Mekong River Commission, Vientiane. [26]

MRC (2018), "Development of Guidelines for Hydropower Environmental Impact Mitigation and Risk Management in the Lower Mekong Mainstream and Tributaries", Mekong River Commission, Vientiane. [19]

MRC (2018), "Irrigation Database Improvement for the Lower Mekong Basin", Mekong River Commission, Vientiane. [6]

MRC (2018), "Mekong Climate Change Adaptation Strategy and Action Plan", Mekong River Commission, Vientiane. [44]

MRC (2018), "MRC Council Study: Flood Sector Key Findings Report", Mekong River Commission, Vientiane. [34]

MRC (2018), "State of the Basin Report", Mekong River Commission, Vientiane. [7]

MRC (2017), "The Council Study: Report for Navigation Thematic Area", Mekong River Commission, Vientiane. [18]

MRC (2017), "Transboundary Fisheries Management Issues–In the Mekong and Sekong Rivers of Cambodia and Lao PDR", Mekong River Commission, Vientiane. [28]

MRC (2016), "Basin Development Strategy 2016-2020", Mekong River Commission, Ventiane. [10]

MRC (2015), "Fisheries Research and Development in the Mekong Region", *Catch and Culture*, Mekong River Commission, pp. 4-7, http://www.mrcmekong.org/news-and-events/events/mrc-updated-database-offers-comprehensive-information-on-mekong-fish-species/. [27]

MRC (2012), *Navigation Programme 2013-2015: Programme Document*, Mekong River Commission, Vientiane, http://www.mrcmekong.org/assets/Publications/Programme-Documents/NAP-2013-2015-Programme-Document.pdf. [14]

MRC (2010), "State of River", Mekong River Commission, Vientiane. [3]

MRC (2009), "Cambodia and Viet Nam formally open-up cross-border river trade on the Mekong", Press release, 9 December, Mekong River Commission, Vientiane, http://www.mrcmekong.org/news-and-events/news/cambodia-and-viet-nam-formally-open-up-cross-border-river-trade-on-the-mekong/. [17]

Neiland, A. and C. Béné (2008), "Tropical river fisheries valuation: Background papers to a global synthesis", *The WorldFish Center Studies and Reviews*, The World Fish Centre Studies and Reviews, Penang. [36]

Oeurng, C. et al. (2019), "Assessing Climate Change Impacts on River Flows in the Tonle Sap Lake Basin, Cambodia", *Water*, Vol. 11/3, p. 618, http://dx.doi.org/10.3390/w11030618. [2]

Open Development Mekong (2017), *"Open Development Mekong – Hydropower dams"*, https://opendevelopmentmekong.net/topics/hydropower/ (accessed on 13 May 2020). [23]

Sassoon, A. (2017), "Cambodia's fisheries at risk due to hydropower development on Mekong, MRC warns", *Phnom Penh Post*, https://www.phnompenhpost.com/national/cambodias-fisheries-risk-due-hydropower-development-mekong-mrc-warns. [20]

Sebesvari, Z. and F. Renaud (2017), "What Mekong Delta communities can teach us about access to safe water", United Nations University Sustainable Development Explorer, https://ourworld.unu.edu/en/what-mekong-delta-communities-can-teach-us-about-access-to-safe-water. [11]

Sembiring, M. (2018), "Examining Cooperation for Climate Change Adaptation in Southeast Asia: The Case of Lower Mekong River Basin", *NTS Insight*, No. IN18-03, RSIS Centre for Non-Traditional Security Studies, Singapore, https://www.rsis.edu.sg/wp-content/uploads/2018/04/NTS-insight-Technology-Applications-in-Climate-Change-Adaptation-Regime-LMB-Case.pdf. [45]

Seng, R. (2019), "Livelihoods in the changing Tonle Sap: Past, present and future", Biodiversity and Ecology, Université Paul Sabatier – Toulouse III, 30 August. [37]

Smajgl, A. and J. Ward (eds.) (2013), *The Water-Food-Energy Nexus in the Mekong Region*, Springer New York, http://dx.doi.org/10.1007/978-1-4614-6120-3. [13]

UNECE (2019), "Inland Water Transport in Europe: Addressing the 2030 Agenda for Sustainable Development, Next Steps and Recommendations", Economic Commission for Europe, Inland Transport Committee, Working Party on Inland Water Transport, https://www.unece.org/fileadmin/DAM/trans/doc/2019/sc3/ECE-TRANS-SC.3-2019-03e_final.pdf. [15]

UNECE and INBO (2015), *Water and Climate Change Adaptation in Transboundary Basins: Lessons Learned and Good Practices*, United Nations Economic Commission For Europe, Geneva and International Network of Basin Organizations, Paris, https://www.unece.org/fileadmin/DAM/env/water/publications/WAT_Good_practices/ece.mp.wat.45.pdf. [41]

UNFCCC (2018), "How hydropower can help climate action", *UN Climate Change News*, United Nations Framework Convention on Climate Change, https://unfccc.int/news/how-hydropower-can-help-climate-action. [25]

UNWTO (2016), *Mekong River-based Tourism Product Development*, World Tourism Organization (UNWTO), http://dx.doi.org/10.18111/9789284418015. [40]

Vannak, C. (2017), "Fish yields rise, exports fall", *Khmer Times*, https://www.khmertimeskh.com/60519/fish-yields-rise-exports-fall/ (accessed on 13 May 2020). [29]

Vu, T. and M. Mayer (2018), "Hydropower infrastructure and regional order making in the Sub-Mekong region", *Revista Brasileira de Política Internacional*, Vol. 61/1, http://dx.doi.org/10.1590/0034-7329201800114. [21]

WWF (2017), "New Species Discoveries in 2016", World Wide Fund for Nature, https://greatermekong.panda.org/discovering_the_greater_mekong/species/new_species/stranger_species/. [5]

WWF (2009), *The Greater Mekong and Climate Change: Biodiversity, Ecosystem Services and Development at Risk*, World Wildlife Fund, Gland, Switzerland, https://www.wwf.de/fileadmin/fm-wwf/Publikationen-PDF/greater_mekong_climate_change_report.pdf. [35]

WWF (n.d.), "A biological treasure trove", https://greatermekong.panda.org/discovering_the_greater_mekong/ (accessed on 13 May 2020). [4]

WWF-Greater Mekong (2018), *Sands Are Running Out*, WWF–Greater Mekong, Bangkok, https://www.wwf.org.uk/sites/default/files/2018-04/180419_Mekong_sediment_CS-external.pdf. [38]

WWF-Greater Mekong (2016), *Mekong River in the Economy*, WWF–Greater Mekong, Bangkok, https://wwfasia.awsassets.panda.org/downloads/mekong_river_in_the_economy_final.pdf. [1]

XinhuaNet (2019), *"China Focus: Joint patrols on Mekong revitalize 'golden waterway'"*, http://www.xinhuanet.com/english/2019-11/24/c_138579268.htm (accessed on 13 May 2020). [46]

XinhuaNet (2018), *"73rd joint patrol on Mekong River starts"*, http://www.xinhuanet.com/english/2018-08/21/c_137408042.htm (accessed on 13 May 2020). [47]

Xu, H., J. Bao and C. Zhou (2006), "Effectiveness of regional tourism integration", *Chinese Geographical Science*, Vol. 16/2, pp. 141-147, http://dx.doi.org/10.1007/s11769-006-0008-3. [43]

2 The potential of digital infrastructure financing: Fintech and blockchain

The public sector continues to finance the bulk of infrastructure in Asia and the Mekong region, although the private sector is increasingly involved through public-private partnerships (PPPs) and privatisation. This chapter explores alternative finance mechanisms that harness digital technologies (e.g. Fintech) to fund infrastructure, including crowdfunding and tokenisation. It suggests such platforms can help transcend the limits of traditional banks, providing a lower entry cost for retail investors. They can also build community support, sending a reassuring signal to larger institutional investors. The chapter also highlights the use of crowdfunding and blockchain tokens to support a variety of projects, including in real estate, energy, parks, transport and water. Despite these successful case studies, the use of Fintech to finance public infrastructure remains marginal.

Introduction

The private sector is increasingly engaged in financing infrastructure in Asia, primarily through partnerships with the public sector and via privatisation, though the public sector continues to fund most infrastructure in the region. Alternative finance mechanisms are emerging, however, that harness digital technologies (e.g. Fintech) to fund infrastructure. Such platforms, including crowdfunding and tokenisation, can help transcend the limits of traditional banks, providing a lower entry cost for retail investors. They can also demonstrate community interest, sending a reassuring signal to larger institutional investors. This chapter highlights the use of crowdfunding and blockchain tokens to support a variety of projects, including in real estate, energy, parks, transport, and particularly water. Despite several success stories, the use of digital platforms to finance infrastructure is in its infancy.

The infrastructure financing gap calls for alternative and innovative funding channels

Asia, including the Mekong region, has substantial financing needs for physical infrastructure, but struggles to obtain suitable funding from sources beyond the public sector (OECD, 2018[1]). The gap is particularly glaring in less-developed economies in the region relative to their economic size (Asian Development Bank, 2017[2]). Asia needs more alternative and innovative channels to fill this gap in infrastructure funding.

The public sector still accounts for the largest share in capital outlays (Hansakul and Levinger, 2016[3]; UN ESCAP, 2017[4]). 70% of Asian infrastructure funding comes directly from the public sector. The private sector contributes 20%, while multilateral agencies, such as international development banks, provide the remainder (Aladdin D. and Zulfiqar, 2017[5]). In Asia, the public sector participates in infrastructure financing by drawing from tax and non-tax revenues, as well as borrowing (e.g. national and municipal bonds). Governments also draw on loans from multilateral institutions to augment the fund pool.

The private sector invests in infrastructure mostly through bank loans

Private-sector participation in infrastructure (PPI) comes mainly through privatisation and public-private partnerships (PPPs). Table 2.1 shows that the percentage of private ownership in publicly awarded projects is now effectively equal among the world's regions. Transport projects in sub-Saharan Africa have a lower private ownership share than those in other regions. Emerging economies in Asia and in Latin America and the Caribbean have private ownership shares in excess of 95%, while other regions have average shares between 90% and 92%. Emerging economies in Asia and in Latin America and the Caribbean have larger proportions of projects in land transport as a segment of the transportation sector. Conversely, in other regions, less than half of transport projects are for land transport. The Middle East and North Africa region does not have any land transport projects in the database for the selected financial closure timeframe.

Table 2.2 indicates an increase in average project size for all countries in Asia, except Malaysia. Cambodia's USD 1 billion investment in transport PPI is for a single airport project. Sectoral information is not available for Lao People's Democratic Republic (hereafter "Lao PDR"), while subsector-level data are absent for Myanmar. Thailand has a pair of railway projects in the database. Indonesia has allocated nearly half of its outlay for a single rail project, while using the remainder for road projects.

Private sector participation leans more on the debt market, especially bank lending. Commercial bank loans, specifically syndicated loans, are the primary mechanism to fund infrastructure; the bond market is still developing (Yoshino, Helble and Abidhadjaev, 2018[6]). Equity issuance and corporate bonds represent another source, mostly for entities directly involved in infrastructure sectors such as utilities, transportation and mining. Several listed infrastructure companies in the region and Asia-focused infrastructure equity indices have a relatively strong presence in the market.[1] Their unlisted counterparts are also gaining some attention.

Institutional investors such as sovereign wealth funds, pension funds, and insurance companies have increasing interest in infrastructure as an asset, but current policy fails to encourage this mechanism (Yoshino, Helble and Abidhadjaev, 2018[6]). Investor regulation is deemed to be one of the primary constraints. The market for securities is also generally at an early stage of development in many countries.

Table 2.1. Infrastructure project with private sector participation (by region), 2010-19

Number of projects	All projects	Transport	Land transport
Emerging economies in Asia	2 013	529	469
Europe and Central Asia	459	55	28
Latin America and the Caribbean	946	185	117
Middle East and North Africa	102	4	0
Sub-Saharan Africa	234	25	9
Investment in USD billion	**All projects**	**Transport**	**Land transport**
Emerging economies in Asia	416.6	183.2	165.5
Europe and Central Asia	167.9	84.9	38.9
Latin America and the Caribbean	300.8	119.6	79.5
Middle East and North Africa	21.9	1.3	0.0
Sub-Saharan Africa	54.1	11.5	2.0
Average private ownership, percentage	**All projects**	**Transport**	**Land transport**
Emerging economies in Asia	96.9	95.8	96.8
Europe and Central Asia	95.2	91.6	90.7
Latin America and the Caribbean	96.2	98.2	99.9
Middle East and North Africa	97.8	90.8	-
Sub-Saharan Africa	94.7	91.4	90.1

Note: Not all projects have data on investment level and/or private ownership. Average private ownership only considers projects for which data are available. The years refer to financial closure years listed in the World Bank PPI Database.
Source: World Bank PPI Database.

Table 2.2. Infrastructure projects with private sector participation by sector in Emerging Asia, 2010-19

	Average investment by project, USD billion					
	All projects		Transport		Land transport	
	2007-16	2010-19	2007-16	2010-19	2007-16	2010-19
Cambodia	0.18	0.37	-	1.00	-	0.00
China	0.08	0.15	0.46	0.48	0.71	0.52
India	0.22	0.23	0.16	0.25	0.16	0.24
Indonesia	0.29	0.74	0.22	1.50	0.24	1.50
Lao PDR	0.50	0.78	-	-	-	-
Malaysia	0.37	0.24	0.32	1.54	0.32	-
Myanmar	0.17	0.29	0.06	0.05	-	-
Philippines	0.31	0.35	0.22	0.41	0.32	0.48
Thailand	0.17	0.24	-	1.68	-	1.68
Viet Nam	0.07	0.20	0.12	0.23	0.00	0.38

Note: Not all projects have data on investment level. Average private ownership only considers projects for which data are available. The years refer to financial closure years listed in the World Bank PPI Database.
Source: World Bank PPI Database.

The central role of banks creates challenges

The centrality of banks in funding infrastructure poses three challenges: lending duration, volume of loanable capital and community engagement. First, since banks' loanable funds are largely composed of demand deposits, the tenor of their investments is limited. Second, performance and asset quality ratios demanded of banks in a well-supervised environment limit the volume of loanable capital. Finally, traditional lending by banks gives limited attention to community needs and interests.

Technologies that enable financial intermediation could help narrow the financing gap both directly and indirectly. Such platforms could reach retail investors more efficiently than traditional mechanisms, where the cost of investor entry is high. In its current forms, fundraising through these channels is generally suitable for small-scale infrastructure projects. However, beyond the capital raised, the participation of retail investors in infrastructure finance can be a valuable indicator of the project's social acceptance and future use.

Highly favourable feedback from participating communities could help attract larger institutional investors. When the general public participates in infrastructure fundraising, it can give rise to a new network of trust within the local community (Davis and Cartwright, 2019[7]). It is further posited that engaging local stakeholders from the start is paramount to secure community support and ensure that key messages are communicated well to residents. The extent of community awareness could also enhance transparency for project disbursements.

Technology-enabled financing platforms empower retail investor base

Technology-enabled financing platforms have grown substantially in the last few years. Since the global financial crisis, these platforms have become a popular choice for small projects that would have had difficulty securing capital from traditional creditors. Moreover, they serve as an alternative investment option for individuals with savings.

Crowdfunding

Crowdfunding is one way for individuals, or participants at large, to pool funds to finance businesses, projects, or other needs of enterprises or other individuals (De Buysere et al., 2012[8]; Jenik, Lyman and Nava, 2017[9]). Crowdfunding can take the form of debt, equity, royalty, reward, or donation. However, in some instances, it refers to equity sales to distinguish it from peer-to-peer lending. The online alternative finance market volume in the Asia-Pacific region has grown by a factor of more than 15 since 2014 to more than EUR 320 billion in 2017. This dwarfs the volume in Europe and the Americas. The People's Republic of China (hereafter "China") accounted for over 99% of the total volume in the Asia-Pacific region (Ziegler et al., 2019[10]).

In crowdfunding, fundraising mainly involves the investor, the capital recipient or the borrower, and the marketplace platform (Figure 2.1). The link between the investor and the capital recipient is more direct compared to the banking system (Box 2.1). Crowdfunding instruments can either be equity, debt or loan, or donation. In lending transactions (also called peer-to-peer lending), loan originators are also part of the equation; in many cases, they are akin to mortgage brokers. The loan originator can be a bank or a non-bank financial institution that seeks out borrowers willing and eligible to raise funds in the marketplace. The loan originators are effectively sellers of the loans. However, unlike in bank lending, the investors are the ones bearing the direct credit risk. At most, buyback guarantees are made available in certain cases, wherein the originator covers or buys the loan in the event of non-payment by the borrower. To facilitate mutual understanding, the platforms set the rules of engagement. They also release the project information of the proponents (for equity and donation), provide credit risk assessment to investors (for loans) and facilitate payment, clearing and settlement. There are platforms that also provide access to a secondary market. This allows investors to dispose of their assets subject to regulations governing the platform – even before the date of maturity in the case of loans.

Figure 2.1. Basic crowdfunding model (simplified representation)

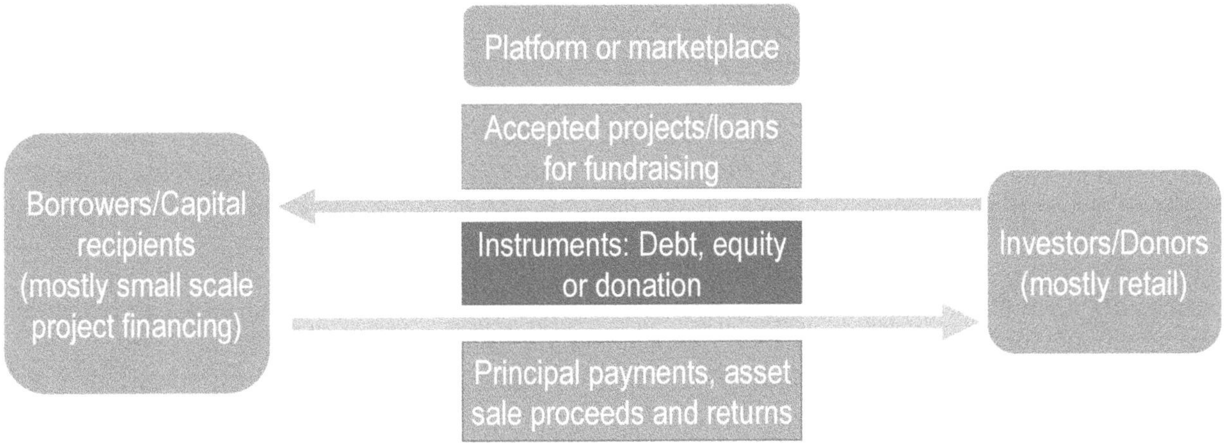

Source: Authors.

Box 2.1. Traditional bank lending

Banks' lending operations are generally funded by short-term deposits (Figure 2.2). In certain countries in Asia, banks offer their depositors an interest on their deposits to incentivise placements. Deposit insurance is also used to protect the depositors to some degree in case of a bank run. On the other hand, lending rates are charged by banks on borrowers. To mitigate risk taking, the central bank typically imposes a reserve requirement ratio that sets the amount of deposit reserves that banks should maintain in a fractional reserve system. This is accompanied by other mandated ratios to safeguard banking stability. Another key feature of the traditional banking system is the clear division between banks' deposit-taking and lending operations. This places depositors outside of the banks' lending decisions; thus depositors cannot dictate to banks who can receive loans. The system also does not give the depositors readily available access to the information pertaining to the banks' borrowing clients and their activities.

Figure 2.2. Bank lending model (simplified representation)

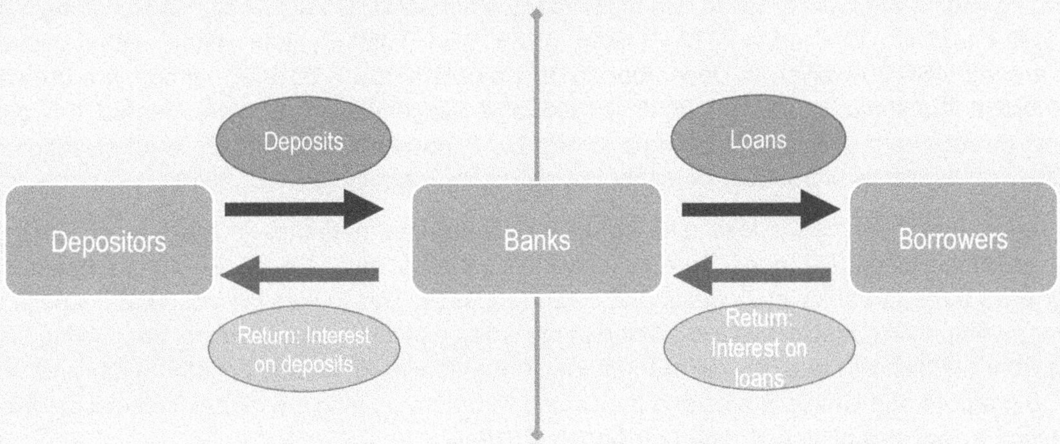

Source: Authors.

Crowdfunding is somewhat similar to the traditional securities markets, such as those for equities and bonds (Figure 2.3). One of the key differences between the two is the cost of entry to participate directly in the primary market activity. Crowdfunding platforms make it easier for small projects or businesses to enter into the marketplace compared to the traditional securities markets, despite the initiatives of the latter to broaden their portfolio of non-large enterprises. Crowdfunding marketplaces customarily have lower investor entry cost than traditional securities markets, albeit online securities trading platforms for retail investors have proliferated. Additionally, the investors know of specific projects as opposed to general corporate needs in the traditional securities markets; recent innovations such as infrastructure bonds might be an exception. Effectively, in equity share or civic project donation crowdfunding campaigns, investor participation indicates the degree of community approval, if not support. The credit risk assessment practices are also different. While in the traditional securities market external parties take part in the risk assessment (e.g. underwriting institutions), crowdfunding risk assessment is done by the platform. It is an internal process similar to bank lending risk evaluation, although it may differ in the details of the assessment.

Figure 2.3. Basic equity and bonds market model (simplified representation)

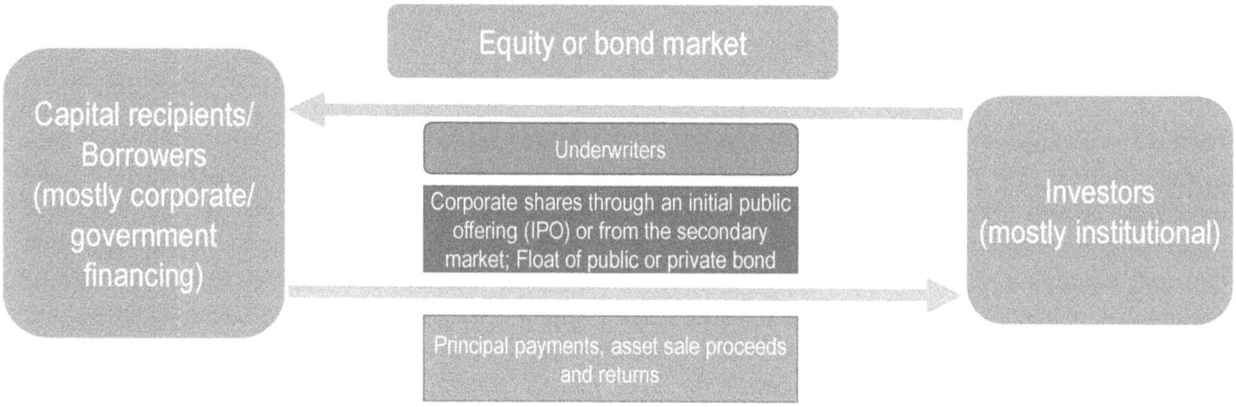

Source: Authors.

Tokenisation

Tokenisation through blockchain carries promise in complementing, if not advancing, the manner of crowdfunding (Box 2.2).[2] Coin or token offerings attracted almost USD 20 billion in capital globally in 2018, up from less than USD 1 million in 2013 (Strategy&, 2019[11]). Total cryptocurrency market capitalisation stood at around USD 200 billion in December 2019 (CoinMarketCap, 2019[12]), although it breached the USD 800 billion threshold in January 2018. Fraud and speculation may have dented the growth in fundraising through coin offerings following a strong 2017; however, the concept of tokenisation can still potentially raise capital for infrastructure either through debt or equity (OECD, 2019[13]).

In essence, tokenisation means less reliance on traditional intermediaries in the flow of funding. After government-issued funds (fiat money) are converted into tokens, payment, clearing and settlement would no longer pass through banks, custodians and clearinghouses. This lowers the cost and financial barriers to investor participation (Uzsoki, 2019[14]). At the same time, relative to crowdfunding, decoupling the ledger of assets from the platform reduces the market power of these intermediaries (Roth, Schär and Schöpfer, 2019[15]). Singapore, the United States and the United Kingdom – being the global financial centres – lead in fundraising by geographic jurisdiction (ICObench, 2019[16]).

Box 2.2. Crowdfunding, tokens and project financing

Crowdfunding can be categorised in two ways, depending on the type of return offered to investors. Financial return-oriented crowdfunding pertains to equity sales that offer possibility of dividends, capital gains from resale in the secondary online market; and to peer-to-peer lending with a pre-set interest rate and tenor. Non-financial return-oriented crowdfunding pertains to donations and capital raising in exchange for non-financial rewards (e.g. publicising names of donors or giving out tokens of appreciation). The latter is usually associated with community-led or civic initiatives. In these cases, crowdfunding becomes a tool to gauge the sentiment of community members about the project.

In a way, fundraising through blockchain is a tokenised version of crowdfunding. Blockchain technology-based projects generally offer utility or financial security through tokens to raise financing. Utility tokens, largely issued through initial coin offerings (ICOs) and initial exchange offerings (IEOs), give investors access to protocols or applications. On the other hand, security tokens can take the form of equity in a project, ownership in a certain type of asset like real estate or commodity, or debt. In recent years, this type of equity has been mainly distributed through security token offerings (STOs).

The origins of ICOs can be traced back to 2013 with the issuance of Mastercoin or Omni Layer (Lahajnar and Rožanec, 2018[17]). ICO fundraising has picked up since then, particularly in 2017, though the sentiment has subsided and oscillated since then. Between February 2014 and October 2018, the cumulative value of ICOs rose by over a factor of 12 500 to over USD 22 billion (CoinDesk, 2019[18]). The number of ICOs and the average amount of capital raised per ICO increased sharply during this period. ICOs cover mainly utility tokens, though there are grey area cases (i.e. difficulty in distinguishing whether a token is for utility or an asset). Utility tokens are viewed as a way for start-ups to take advantage of relatively lighter regulations to raise funds. This is because ICO placements may not be classified as investments, but as donations (Ante and Fiedler, 2019[19]).

Security tokens were first offered in 2017, when Blockchain Capital tokenised its investment fund (Newtown Partners, 2019[20]). Broadly, this category includes the financial rights to instruments such as equity, debt and dividends, as well as rights to profit sharing, voting and buyback. Identifying asset categories had been contentious in the past, owing to implications on regulatory compliance. It took an investigation from the US Securities Commission to declare the tokens issued by *The Dao* as securities (US SEC, 2017[21]). However, as failures hound ICOs, regulatory oversight became an attractive feature of STOs' credibility. The underlying blockchain technology in STOs is noted for transparency and pseudo-anonymity; transactions and ownership are broadcast to the network (Ante and Fiedler, 2019[19]). Cumulative fundraising has risen by more than a factor of 30 to over USD 330 million since the Blockchain Capital issuance (Newtown Partners, 2019[20]).

Meanwhile, IEO was introduced to the market in late 2017. In IEO, a crypto-centralised exchange platform conducts an ICO on the exchange as opposed to on the issuer's platform. This mode essentially merges the fundraising and listing process, interposing the exchanges between the token issuer and the investors. IEOs effectively re-introduced centralisation in the vetting process, where exchanges serve as evaluators of projects. While relatively nascent compared to traditional ICOs and STOs, capital raising through IEOs gained considerable momentum in 2019 (Strategy&, 2019[11]). In the first half of 2019, IEO projects collected more than USD 1.6 billion (Inwara, 2019[22]).

From the above snapshot, the market is leaning towards a more reassuring system that considers the extent of information asymmetry. Myalo and Glukhov (2019[23]) provide a useful comparison of these modes. Nonetheless, failures still happen, including those already listed in exchanges. Indeed, exchanges themselves crash. With this backdrop, governments in Asia are fast-tracking regulations pertaining to digital coins. Understandably, the coverage and tightness of these regulations vary in many respects across countries. China, Hong Kong (China), Korea, the Philippines, Singapore and Thailand, among others, have released new regulatory guidelines (Lewis and Cheng, 2019[24]; Ezquer, 2020[25]). A number of outstanding regulatory issues remain, pertaining to listing, trading, custody, post-trading and fraud clearance (Deloitte, 2019[26]). Since digital coins involve cross-border transactions, collaboration in the delivery of regulations is vital.

Tokenisation in the context of infrastructure divides the value of assets or the underlying securities (debt or equity) into smaller parcels before they are offered to potential investors. The basic set-up is depicted by Figure 2.4. The tokens come in digital format to represent a claim on the physical asset or security. They are launched on blockchains guided by the terms of the smart contracts. The smart contracts backstop the creation of the tokens and outline their characteristics. The newly created digital tokens are usually purchased with another token, typically that of the host blockchain. The Ethereum ecosystem, for instance, is a commonly used launchpad for the new tokens wherein *ether* is used as the native token. Notably, tokens can also be exchanged for either another token or fiat currency (where the legal system permits) in token exchanges. Custody of tokens is either through a hard wallet or digital wallets built into the trading exchange, host blockchain or a third party service provider. Blockchain applications such as tokenisation are deemed to foster liquidity in an asset market that is customarily illiquid, such as real estate (Smith et al., 2019[27]). Moreover, tokens carry relatively lower transaction costs than traditional securities; their digital nature makes their usage more efficient, while blockchain technology enhances transparency (Uzsoki, 2019[14]). Much like crowdfunding, tokenisation of assets or projects also directly involves participating investors.

Figure 2.4. Basic tokenisation model (simplified representation)

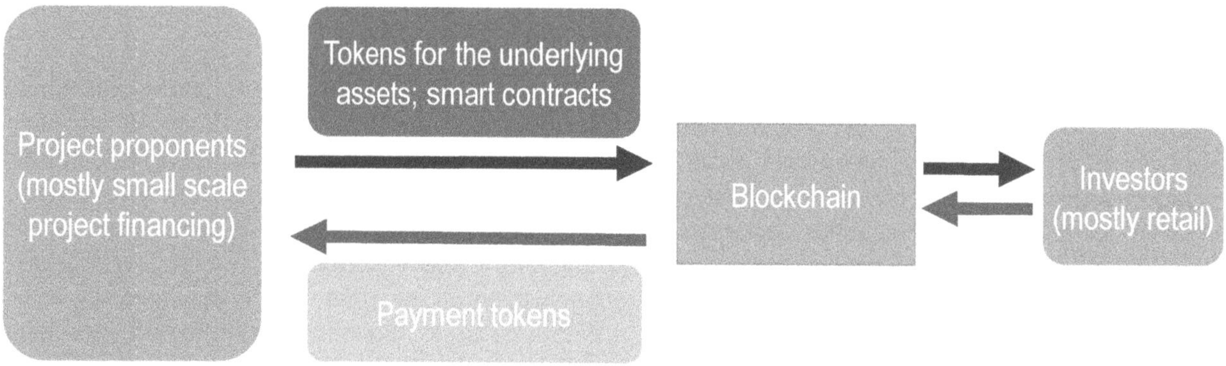

Source: Authors.

Risk assessment

The adequacy of risk assessment, particularly for large transactions like infrastructure projects, is a key consideration in promoting alternative finance. Infrastructure as an asset typically has substantial upside. However, the experience of banks in India indicates it can also be a drag on the balance sheet of lenders if vetting is weak. Based on the Indian central bank's data, the stressed advances ratio of banks to the infrastructure sector rose to over 22% in March 2018, before falling to slightly less than 18% in March 2019 (RBI, 2019[28]). The participation of local government in raising capital through alternative finance platforms demands a sound framework. This can mitigate the accumulation of contingent liabilities on the part of national governments. The existence and depth of secondary markets for transactions coursed through alternative channels is another important factor to exploit in broadening the use of these platforms in an effective manner.

Private projects are getting a boost from alternative platforms

The variety of projects financed through crowdfunding and blockchain tokens is quite extensive. Crowdfunding has supported projects in agriculture, arts, health, fashion, retail goods, comics, technology, etc. (Gałkiewicz and Gałkiewicz, 2018[29]; Huang et al., 2018[30]). Capital inflow from coin offerings is spread across similar domains. This is the case despite the heavy concentration of funding in digital platforms and digital infrastructure related to finance and business services in 2018 (ICObench, 2019[16]).

Private real estate

Crowdfunding is emerging as one of the key sources of debt funding for private real estate developments in the Asia-Pacific region (PWC and Urban Land Institute, 2018[31]). Figure 2.5 shows a trend of growth in this market. Crowdfunding also expands access to investment opportunities in commercial real estate. In the past, real estate investment was almost entirely residential, often the home the investor lived in. Real estate crowdfunding lowers the cost of entry into the real estate market. People previously unable to invest in real estate due to the high initial costs will now be able to do so.

The region has also launched tokens that give direct interest in property projects and to those linked to real estate investment trust funds (REITs). The investment market for real estate – which, as described by Don et al. (2019[32]), is immense but dominated by a closed network of firms and hampered by transactional friction and opacity – is poised to extract gains from tokenisation. Most campaigns for durable capital outlays, including those related to utilities, are for private projects and partly for community-driven or civic projects.

Tokenisation of real estate assets is particularly being pushed in developed economies. An example of this is Aspen coin, which was issued to sell equity of an already operational St. Regis Aspen Resort in Colorado (Carroll, 2018[33]; Kennelly, 2018[34]). Investors in the resort had to be accredited and meet the minimum level of investment. In 2018, an apartment in New York was also tokenised to offer fractional ownership to the project (Wolfson, 2018[35]; Zhao, 2018[36]). Ownership in a South Carolina student housing complex was being partially tokenised in 2018 through a REIT; however, the deal broke down due to disagreements (Young, 2018[37]; Marek, 2019[38]). Meanwhile, the United Kingdom rolled out its first real-estate-backed STO in October 2019 (Bloomberg, 2019[39]); this is estimated to tokenise USD 640 million worth of projects over the next few years.

Figure 2.5. Global real estate crowdfunding market size

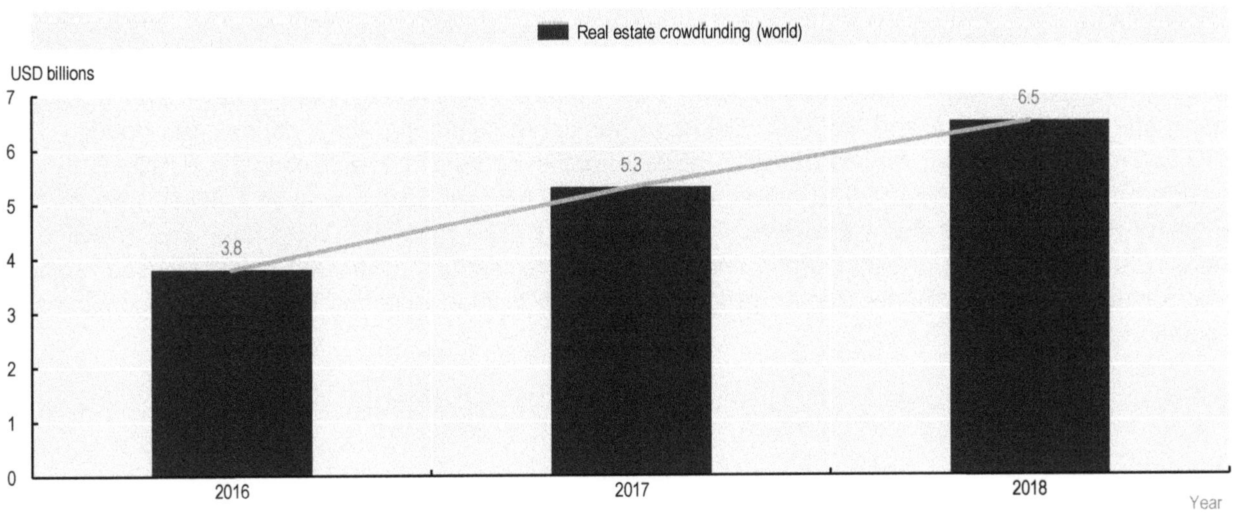

StatLink https://doi.org/10.1787/888934167600

Source: Global Real Estate Crowdfunding (adopted from EY, March (2019[40])).

Energy, parks and transport

Apart from real estate, fundraising through alternative financial platforms has supported projects related to power supply, water management, parks, roads and bicycle lanes, among others. Specialised platforms also link investors and specific undertakings (e.g. solar energy projects). WeShareSolar facilitates crowdfunding for solar energy projects by investing in solar shares in the Netherlands (Smart City Embassy, n.d.[41]). Citizenergy provides an avenue for cross-border investment in sustainable energy projects; most of its funded campaigns are in the European Union and partly in Africa (Citizenergy, n.d.[42]).

InfraShares is a US-based platform similar to Citizenergy, but with a wider target coverage. This includes roads, bridges, airports, schools and mass transit, in addition to water systems and renewable energy (InfraShares, n.d.[43]). The portfolio of projects, however, is still limited to one successful campaign to date: Matrix Materials Working Capital Loan for Fairfax County Pilot Projects. Matrix Materials Inc., an Australian firm, secured a loan for USD 40 000 through InfraShares. It was intended to jumpstart the road paving projects in Fairfax County, Virginia, using waste materials. The loan has a tenor of six months and carries an interest rate of 6%.

In 2019, over 1 000 people crowdfunded to buy an 800-hectare plot of wilderness that was being sold by its private owner in Princess Louisa Inlet, British Columbia, Canada. The land is rich in mature conifers and was likely to be sold to a logging firm. However, thanks to the charitable efforts of the BC Parks Foundation, the participants met the CAD 3 million asking price. The wilderness will be retained first as private land, and eventually integrated into neighbouring Crown (government) land as a provincial park. A private entrepreneur provided the final CAD 100 000 to meet the goal on the final day of the crowdfunding campaign.

Crowdfunding for transport infrastructure and real estate

Crowdfunding and tokenisation remain marginal as methods to finance public infrastructure. They are mainly used for last-mile needs and are largely based on donations. Nonetheless, progress in using alternative financing schemes to develop transport power, water projects, and real estate could set the stage for broader usage of these platforms in general public infrastructure financing in the coming years. The United States hosts most of the current instances of these practices.

Mini-bonds for general infrastructure

The city of Denver, Colorado, has partly financed public infrastructure through crowdfunding (Gasparro, 2015[44]). Mini-bonds were floated to supplement the general infrastructure fund in 2014 (Box 2.3). The debt papers were rated and sold to Colorado residents, although they cannot be traded. The USD 550 million campaign, run via the city's website, achieved its aim of collecting 2% (USD 12 million) through crowdfunding. About 1 000 individuals invested. The mini-bonds, sold at USD 500 each, had tenors of 9 and 14 years and were rated Aaa by Moody's. The municipal bond float was intended to respond to the tightening of banking and financial market regulations. Over 300 public-focused projects were funded through the Better Denver programme, which include restoring buildings and constructing recreational centres.

Box 2.3. Crowdfunding mini-bonds

Mini-bonds are debt instruments that offer smaller increments compared to traditional bonds. They allow the issuers to directly tap investors, typically retail investors, for a pre-established fixed rate of return and tenor. They are usually issued by small companies, start-ups or enterprises having difficulty securing funds from institutional investors and traditional channels. In some cases, mini-bonds can be viewed as a parcelled version of municipal bonds or mini-bond (Fu, 2016[45]). Mini-bonds are typically issued by sub-national governmental entities for everyday obligations and for projects such as school buildings, sewer systems and highways (US SEC, 2012[46]). Mini-bonds tend to offer high returns considering the much higher investment risks (FCA, 2019[47]). Crowdfunding has become a staple mode to sell mini-bonds in recent years. Even in countries such as the United Kingdom, however, regulations are still catching up (King, 2016[48]). The increasing popularity of the debt paper coupled with perceived opaqueness and high-level of risk has prompted the UK Financial Conduct Authority to ban mass marketing of speculative mini-bonds to retail consumers, effective January 2020 (FCA, 2019[49]).

Crowdfunding for bicycle lanes

In 2014, Denver resorted to donation crowdfunding to generate last-mile financing for the construction of bicycle lanes in the downtown area. The Arapahoe initiative, crowdfunded through the Ioby platform, responds to a plan announced in 2007 to create bicycle facilities and enhance the downtown area. The crowdfunding exceeded its target of USD 35 000, corresponding to more than 22% of the total funding target of USD 155 000. Approximately USD 120 000 was secured from traditional investment. The protected bicycle lane network will be expanded in phases to accommodate the increase in the number of cyclists and to enhance their safety. Beyond the financial windfall, the crowdfunding serves as a barometer of the community's sentiment towards the project (Gasparro, 2015[44]).

The same strategy was employed in the earlier construction of bicycle lanes in Memphis (the Hampline project). The project aimed to bolster activity in the downtown area, which had become lethargic over the years, and to improve its image as a city for bicyclists (Ioby, 2014[50]). The funding exercise in 2013 set a target of USD 4.5 million. Proponents resorted to crowdfunding, partly through the Ioby platform, to fill the remaining gap of more than USD 68 000. They managed to surpass the crowdfunding threshold after a few weeks, attracting donations from over 700 people.

In Boston, Massachusetts, a private citizen crowdfunded nearly USD 7 000 from 180 donors to place potted flowers and traffic cones in the buffer zone of an unprotected bike lane. Shortly after the flowers and cones were put in place, the city added flexible posts, offering protection for riders from vehicular traffic. While city authorities did not cite the private campaign as the catalyst for their action, coverage of the events in *The Boston Globe* implied the municipal government was responding to the campaign. A similar project in a portion of San Francisco, California, on the Tilt crowdfunding platform raised just over USD 900 around the same time for makeshift flexible posts. The city agreed to leave them in place until it could add official ones.

Crowd support inspires local government to finance pedestrian bridge

In the Netherlands, *I Make Rotterdam* used crowdfunding to finance the construction of the 400-metre long Luchtsingel pedestrian bridge in Rotterdam in 2011 (AIA and Massolution, 2013[51]). Deemed by De Voldere and Zeqo (2017[52]) to be the first crowdfunded public infrastructure project in the world, the project raised approximately EUR 100 000 (Max Borka, 2020[53]). In return, the names of the donors who contributed at least EUR 25 were etched on the planks used to construct the bridge. More than 8 000 planks were sold during the fundraising campaign. Akin to the bicycle lane project in Memphis, Tennessee, the crowdfunding outcome became a measure of public support for the project. It was deemed to have helped convince the local government to fund the bulk of the project cost amounting to EUR 4 million, paving the way for completion of the project in the summer of 2015 (The Urban Web, 2016[54]).

Crowdfunding and debt to establish solar farms

A town in the southwest of England (United Kingdom) also resorted to crowdfunding to bankroll the establishment of solar farms. The Swindon Borough Council's campaign, which offered tax-free interest-earning debt, attracted about GBP 1.8 million in five months through the Abundance Investment platform (Davis and Cartwright, 2019[7]). The crowd investment supplemented the Council's own outlay of about GBP 3 million. The project was in line with the town's objective of shifting towards renewable energy.

For its part, the local government of London launched "Crowdfund London" in 2014 for various projects (London Government, 2019[55]). As of this writing, total pledges have amounted to about GBP 4 million. Of this amount, GBP 1.8 million came from the mayor's office and GBP 2.2 million came from the crowd. More than 100 projects had successful campaigns. These include construction and refurbishment of markets, community kitchens, public spaces, gardens and parks, community centres, village halls and small bridges, among others.

Digital infrastructure financing for water-related projects: Case studies

Digital financing based on Fintech and blockchain is already applied to support water-related infrastructure. The following case studies describe such projects – both government and civic initiated – recently implemented in Asia and OECD countries.

The Pitak Project

- Site: Tubao, la Union, Northern Philippines
- Components: Purchasing and installation of a solar-powered deep well pump, water storage, and distribution system
- Total amount: USD 14 000 (approximate)
- Execution: FREZITE

The Pitak Project, a civic/community-driven project led by women, promoted sustainable and regenerative living in the municipality of Tubao, in part through natural building and permaculture. This involved independence from both electricity and water grids. As the community water supply was unreliable, the project envisioned a solar-powered deep well to draw water for both immediate use and storage. To obtain this equipment, the project partnered with a supplier and initiated a crowdfunding campaign. Between 2 March and 16 April 2015, it raised USD 14 211 – 108% of the USD 13 121 target.

Two major success factors were transparency and promotion.

Transparency: While "Earth care" is a widespread concern that generates large amounts of both activism and action, permaculture itself is a niche interest. The blog post announcing the campaign was concise (under 1 000 words), but dense with information. It addressed the philosophy of permaculture, and the purpose and precise needs of the project. It outlined steps already taken and where financial assistance was needed. Costs were itemised at the component level, giving donors a transparent view of goal setting and fund allocation. It included a plan for using excess donations of USD 3 192 to buy a tilling machine. This may have also assured donors, but its impact is unclear as the campaign did not reach the level of excess donations.

Promotion: The campaign went beyond the project blog, and was shared with other outlets with similar interests. These included permaculture or alternative agriculture; Earth care; and poverty alleviation, especially among marginalised groups. Also, niche celebrities made videos to endorse the campaign. These promotion efforts allowed the campaign to increase the pool of potential donors beyond word-of-mouth. At the same time, they could target donors more likely to be interested than the general population, or even the population of those willing to support crowdfunding campaigns as a whole.

Water purification

- Site: Branson, Colorado, United States
- Components: Purchasing and installation of water filtration system
- Total amount: USD 100 000 (crowdfunding and grants)
- Execution: Innovative Water Technologies

In Branson, Colorado, crowdfunding was used to install a water purification system. This remote community (population 55 in 2019) is close to several springs, so a pump-free water system feeds the town and nearby agricultural land. However, the springs were deemed at risk of surface water contamination, requiring changes. Despite the need for regulatory compliance, the state government did not make traditional funding available (Simpson, 2019[56]). Consequently, Branson sought alternative finance.

The town partnered with a company specialising in filtration on small projects, which provided the system with USD 76 000. Donations ranging from USD 10 to USD 5 000 came from locals, other American residents and community organisations. Media coverage even mentioned a donation from a Branson native living in England (United Kingdom).

The campaign raised under one-third of its USD 100 000 goal. However, the effort, along with the decision to power the system off-grid using solar and wind energy, qualified the project for several government grants to cover the shortfall. In awarding the grants, authorities noted the crowdfunding aspect of the project met or exceeded the matching contribution required, and also made the project more attractive to decision makers.

This is a critical example of how crowdfunding, albeit secondarily, can signal local desire to stimulate political will for a project. It may serve as a model for other infrastructure projects in communities that feel neglected politically (though this may not actually be the case) and are likely facing more imminent needs for development.

Improving water quality in an Aboriginal community

- Site: Buttah Windee, Mid-West Region, West Australia, Australia
- Components: Purchasing and installation of a solar photovoltaic panel-powered hygroscopic water collection system, storage and distribution. Funds diverted to reverse-osmosis water purification system after donation
- Total amount: AUD 26 000 (Australian dollar)
- Execution: Zero Mass Water

In Buttah Windee, Australia, a crowdfunded water infrastructure project is credited with helping save lives, and also preserving the liberty of a marginalised community. Despite having been on their land for generations, the Aboriginal community in mid-western Australia has only been legally recognised since 1993.

Unsafe levels of uranium in the water supply appeared in 2009 and began to displace the community. Ingestion of uranium has been demonstrated to cause multiple forms of organ damage, or organ failure, as well as to increase the risk of cancers or of producing offspring with birth defects.

The state government considered the problem too costly to fix, offering instead to help the remaining families to resettle. In response, a local couple reached out to a company offering a technology to draw water vapour from air. The technology relies on solar hydropanels. Fans take in air, and an absorbent material extracts water vapour from that air. Solar heat then converts the water vapour into pure liquid water, which is finally mineralised for taste and stored.

The couple started a crowdfunding campaign to bear the costs. However, upon learning about the community's dire situation, the company donated the solar panels free of charge. The crowdfund, which had reached AUD 26 000, was diverted to fund construction of a reverse-osmosis water treatment plant. This allowed for further expansion of the safe water supply and development of a fish farm. The fish farm, in turn, provides nutrition and employment to the community, along with a source of external income. The community has been able to stay on their ancestral lands, preserving their way of life and traditions. With this in mind, it is reasonable to call the crowdfunding endeavour a success, even if the target amount is unknown, as it was not mentioned by the source. As in other examples, the key to success in this project was a desire or need expressed by the community.

Water for Arubot

- Site: Arubot, Kavrepanchok District, Nepal
- Components: Pre-feasibility study, feasibility study and implementation
- Total amount: THB (Thai baht) 100 000 combined for the studies

Arubot, a village of approximately 400 people located 90 kilometres west of Kathmandu, lacks reliable water supply. The village relies solely on rainfall, although it is located 600 metres from a river. A group of trekkers heard about the difficult situation from members of the village who work as guides. They devised a three-phase plan to help them secure a water supply: a pre-feasibility study, a feasibility study and implementation. In the pre-feasibility study, the group will visit the village to gain an understanding of the water source, water demand, rough geographical estimates and other available resources. They will use this knowledge to develop a short list of potential technologies to solve the issue. A robust feasibility study will develop detailed plans of needed infrastructure such as amounts and types of tanks, pumps and pipes.

A cost-benefit analysis will also be undertaken. If the plan meets community approval, the project will proceed to implementation, which will require a second round of fundraising. Non-governmental organisations with relevant expertise will be consulted in all phases of this project. As of 6 March 2020, the crowdfunding on GoGetFunding had raised THB 38 450. The crowdfund owner reported that the site visit for the pre-feasibility study occurred on 28-29 December 2019. (No further updates are available at the time of writing.).

Flint Community Water Lab

- Site: Flint, Michigan, United States
- Components: Water quality testing laboratory
- Total amount: USD 70 000 (USD 35 000 crowdfunded, plus USD 35 000 matching grant)
- Execution: Evergreen and Freshwater Future

The Flint water crisis began in spring 2014, when a change in the water source for the city of Flint, Michigan, led to bacterial contamination of the drinking water supply. Further complicating matters, the change of source also led to a change in oversight. The newly appointed officials neglected to include (non-toxic) corrosion inhibitor in the water supply, resulting in the leaching of lead and other toxic metals into the water supply. Many people became either acutely or chronically ill. Twelve deaths are attributed to the crisis, though this number does not include the long-term mortality effects of heavy metal exposure. After trust in public officials was broken, two advocacy groups worked to establish an independent laboratory to test water quality. Following a successful pilot programme in the summer of 2018, the organisations crowdfunded USD 35 000 through Patroncity for a full-scale programme in North Flint, the most-affected area of the city. Local residents would receive job training to operate and staff the laboratory, located in the North Flint community centre. This would allow them to parlay their concern for the community into a career. Water testing would be offered to local residents free of charge (and to others in surrounding areas at a cost). Open House days would allow them to visit and learn about the facility, thereby maintaining transparency. The campaign lasted from 6 May to 1 August 2019. Reaching the goal on 31 July 2019 qualified the project for a matching grant from the Michigan Economic Development Corporation, a PPP. This grant covered the remainder of the cost, which was undisclosed. The laboratory opened in March 2020, and donors of USD 25 or more had their names posted on a wall of the laboratory, either in a general list or with an individual plaque depending on their donation level.

Water Vending Machine

- Site: Ngomai, Tanzania
- Components: Paid-use water pump
- Total amount: EUR 16 000
- Execution: A local entrepreneur with Simavi and Ufundiko

In the community of Ngomai, Tanzania, pumps frequently run dry, forcing women to walk for hours to retrieve water that may not be potable, at the expense of their health and education. A local entrepreneur designed a smart water pump that dispenses water for a small, manageable fee from a "water vending machine". The fee is used to self-finance the maintenance of the pump. The fee is paid by means of coins or tokens that dispense the precise amount to fill a standard water can. A group of local women set the price, and free tokens are distributed to those who cannot afford to pay. This ensures the entire community of approximately 7 000 people benefit from the system. The pump is solar-powered, and excess solar energy stored in batteries allows the pump to provide lighting in the area, protecting the women collecting water after dark. The excess solar energy also allows the pump to play messages recorded by local celebrities that educate the community on health and safety matters. The pump collects accurate data on users and revenues, which are recorded on an online dashboard. This will also notify the community if water is lost to leakage or if the pump is malfunctioning in some way. The entrepreneur trains local workers to make minor repairs to the machine, for which they are paid. People benefitting from this training can also apply their knowledge in other areas, possibly opening up a career path. The fund raised EUR 17 690 in the second half of 2018 on the entrepreneur's own platform.

Building dams to address water scarcity

Pakistan's Supreme Court used crowdfunding to help build the Diamer-bhasha and Mohmand dams (Supreme Court of Pakistan, 2019[57]; The Nation, 2019[58]). The construction of the dams, which aims to alleviate water scarcity in the country, is estimated at close to USD 20 billion. The sizeable amount does not augur well with the national government's austerity measures (Janjua, 2018[59]). Proposed in July 2018, a dam fund, which can be easily tracked by donors on the Supreme Court website, was established to receive proceeds. The website also doubles as a portal for donations. Nearly PKR 11.4 billion (Pakistani rupee), or roughly USD 73.2 million, have been contributed as of 21 November 2019. These contributions have come from both the public and private sectors, including Pakistanis living overseas (The Nation, 2019[58]).

Conclusion

Asia needs more innovative channels to fill its gap in infrastructure funding. In response, alternative mechanisms are emerging that harness digital technologies (Fintech) to fund infrastructure. Such platforms, including crowdfunding and tokenisation, can help transcend the limits of traditional banks, providing a lower entry cost for retail investors. They can also indicate community support, sending a reassuring signal to larger institutional investors.

Fintech has grown substantially in recent years, particularly since the global financial crisis of 2007-08. Crowdfunding, for example, has become a popular choice for small projects that otherwise would have struggled to secure capital from traditional creditors. It has supported projects related to real estate, power supply, water management, parks, roads and bicycle lanes, among others. Fundraising through blockchain is a tokenised version of crowdfunding. By replacing sensitive data with a random number, tokenisation can enhance security, while relying less on traditional intermediaries like banks. For its part, blockchain technology allows for verification without the need for third parties. Tokenisation through blockchain carries promise in complementing, if not advancing, the manner of crowdfunding.

Despite some success stories, the use of crowdfunding and tokenisation to finance public infrastructure remains marginal. It is mainly for last-mile needs and largely based on donations. Nonetheless, progress in using alternative financing schemes to develop real estate, transport, power and water projects could set the stage for broader usage of these platforms in general public infrastructure financing in the coming years. Continued growth of Fintech will depend on adequacy of risk assessment, especially for large transactions like infrastructure projects. The availability and depth of secondary markets for transactions is another important factor to broaden the use of alternative platforms.

References

AIA and Massolution (2013), *Crowdfunding Architecture: Customized Research Report Prepared for the American Institute of Architects*, American Institute of Architects and Massolution, https://neofundproject.files.wordpress.com/2014/09/crowdfunding-architecture.pdf. [51]

Aladdin D., R. and A. Zulfiqar (2017), "Public Financing of Infrastructure in Asia: In Search of New Solutions", Policy Brief, No. 2017-2, Asian Development Bank Institute, https://www.adb.org/publications/public-financing-infrastructure-asia-search-new-solutions. [5]

Ante, L. and I. Fiedler (2019), "Cheap Signals in Security Token Offerings (STOs)", *BRL Working Paper*, Series No. 1, Blockchain Research Lab, http://dx.doi.org/10.2139/ssrn.3356303. [19]

Asian Development Bank (2017), *Meeting Asia's Infrastructure Needs*, Asian Development Bank, Manila, Philippines, http://dx.doi.org/10.22617/fls168388-2. [2]

Bloomberg (2019), "Alliance Investments announces plans to tokenize £500m of UK real estate", *Business*, http://www.bloomberg.com/press-releases/2019-10-30/alliance-investments-announces-plans-to-tokenize-500m-of-uk-real-estate (accessed on 13 May 2020). [39]

Carroll, R. (2018), "In $18 million deal, nearly one-fifth of St. Regis Aspen sells through digital tokens", *Aspen Times*, http://www.aspentimes.com/trending/in-18-million-deal-nearly-one-fifth-of-st-regis-aspen-sells-through-digital-tokens/. [33]

Citizenergy (n.d.), *Projects website*, https://citizenergy.eu/projects (accessed on 24 November 2019). [42]

CoinDesk (2019), *CoinDesk ICO Tracker (database)*, https://www.coindesk.com/ICO-tracker (accessed on 8 March 2020). [18]

CoinMarketCap (2019), *Total Market Capitalization (database)*, https://coinmarketcap.com/charts/ (accessed on 20 December 2019). [12]

Davis, M. and L. Cartwright (2019), *Financing for Society: Assessing the Suitability of Crowdfunding for the Public Sector*, University of Leeds, Leeds, https://doi.org/10.5518/100/7. [7]

De Buysere, K. et al. (2012), *A Framework for European Crowdfunding*, http://eurocrowd.org/wp-content/blogs.dir/sites/85/2013/06/FRAMEWORK_EU_CROWDFUNDING.pdf. [8]

De Voldere, I. and K. Zeqo (2017), *Crowdfunding: Reshaping the Crowd's Engagement in Culture*, European Commission, Brussels, https://europa.eu/capacity4dev/crowdfunding/documents/new-report-crowdfunding-reshaping-crowds-engagement-culture. [52]

Deloitte (2019), *Are Token Assets the Securities of Tomorrow?*, Deloitte, https://www2.deloitte.com/content/dam/Deloitte/lu/Documents/technology/lu-token-assets-securities-tomorrow.pdf. [26]

Don, B. et al. (2019), *Real Estate Use Cases for Blockchain Technology*, Enterprise Ethereum Alliance, Wakefield, Massachusetts, Vol. 1, https://entethalliance.org/wp-content/uploads/2019/05/EEA-Real-Estate-SIG-Use-Cases-May-2019.pdf. [32]

EY (2019), "Real Estate Crowdfunding, Introduction to an alternative way of investing", https://www.ey.com/Publication/vwLUAssets/Real_Estate_Crowdfunding/%24FILE/EY-Real%20Estate%20Crowdfunding-March%202019.pdf. [40]

Ezquer, E. (2020), "Bitcoin regulations by country (updated for 2020)", Bitcoin Market Journal, http://www.bitcoinmarketjournal.com/bitcoin-regulation-by-country/ (accessed on 13 May 2020). [25]

FCA (2019), *"Mini-Bonds", webpage*, http://www.fca.org.uk/consumers/mini-bonds (accessed on 16 December 2019). [47]

FCA (2019), "FCA to ban promotion of speculative mini-bonds to retail consumers", Press Release, 26 November, Financial Conduct Authority, London, http://www.fca.org.uk/news/press-releases/fca-ban-promotion-speculative-mini-bonds-retail-consumers. [49]

Fu, E. (2016), "Mini-bonds: Public engagement and public investment", *Government Finance Review*, October, Chicago, Illinois, http://www.gfoa.org/sites/default/files/GFR101616.pdf. [45]

Gałkiewicz, D. and M. Gałkiewicz (2018), *Crowdfunding Monitor 2018: An Overview of European Projects Financed on Startnext and Kickstarter Platforms between 2010 and mid-2017,*, Bermag, Szczecin, Poland, http://www.fh-kufstein.ac.at/eng/content/download/3541982/file/Crowdfunding_Monitor_2018.pdf. [29]

Gasparro, K. (2015), "Funding municipal infrastructure: Integrating project finance and crowdfunding", Working Paper, Global Project Center, Stanford University, Stanford,, https://gpc.stanford.edu/sites/g/files/sbiybj8226/f/wp87.pdf. [44]

Hansakul, S. and H. Levinger (2016), "Asia infrastructure financing: Getting it right would lift medium-term growth", *Current Issues–Emerging Markets*, Deutsche Bank Research, Frankfurt am Main, http://www.dbresearch.com/PROD/RPS_EN-PROD/PROD0000000000452069/Asia_infrastructure_financing.pdf. [3]

Huang, Z. et al. (2018), "The nature of crowdfunding in China: Initial evidence", *Asia Pacific Journal of Innovation and Entrepreneurship*, Emerald Publishing Limited, Bingley, United Kingdom, pp. 300-322, http://dx.doi.org/10.1108/apjie-08-2018-0046. [30]

ICObench (2019), *ICO Market Analysis 2018*, https://icobench.com/reports/ICO_Market_Analysis_2018.pdf. [16]

InfraShares (n.d.), *"Investments", webpage*, https://invest.infrashares.com/en/explore/projects (accessed on 25 November 2019). [43]

Inwara (2019), *InWara's Blockchain and Crypto Annual Report 2019*, https://www.inwara.com/report/blockchain-crypto-report-h1-2019/. [22]

Ioby (2014), *"The Hampline", webpage*, https://ioby.org/project/hampline (accessed on 20 November 2019). [50]

Janjua, H. (2018), "Crowdfunding for dams – why Pakistani PM Khan's drive is not feasible", Deutsche Welle (DW), Bonn, https://p.dw.com/p/35WC5. [59]

Jenik, I., T. Lyman and A. Nava (2017), "Crowdfunding and financial inclusion", CGAP Working Paper, Consultative Group to Assist the Poor, Washington, D.C., http://www.cgap.org/sites/default/files/Working-Paper-Crowdfunding-and-Financial-Inclusion-Mar-2017.pdf. [9]

Kennelly, C. (2018), "St. Regis Aspen resort raises $18 million via security token offering", Cryptoslate, https://cryptoslate.com/st-regis-aspen-resort-raises-18-million-via-security-token-offering/. [34]

King, C. (2016), "Mini-bonds: Risk and reward?", Eurofenix, Autumn, INSOL Europe, Clifton, United Kingdom, http://www.insol-europe.org/download/documents/864. [48]

Lahajnar, S. and A. Rožanec (2018), "Initial Coin Offering (ICO) evaluation model", *Investment Management and Financial Innovations*, Vol. 15/4, pp. 169-182, http://dx.doi.org/10.21511/imfi.15(4).2018.14. [17]

Lewis, A. and X. Cheng (2019), "The State of Security Token Regulations in Asia", *Opinion*, CoinDesk, http://www.coindesk.com/the-state-of-security-token-regulations-in-asia. [24]

London Government (2019), *"Campaigns We've Backed", webpage*, http://www.london.gov.uk/what-we-do/regeneration/funding-opportunities/crowdfund-london/campaigns-weve-backed-0#acc-i-52927 (accessed on 19 November 2019). [55]

Marek, L. (2019), "DRW real estate token deal falls apart", CRAIN's Chicago Business, http://www.chicagobusiness.com/node/844011/printable/print. [38]

Max Borka (2020), *Design a Bridge–Zus AO–Luchtsingel, webpage*, https://www.maxborka.com/mapping-the-design-world/design-as-a-bridge-zus-ao-luchtsingel/. [53]

Myalo, A. and N. Glukhov (2019), "Comparison Analysis of ICO, DAOICO, IEO and STO. Case Study.", *SSRN Electronic Journal*, http://dx.doi.org/10.2139/ssrn.3447974. [23]

Newtown Partners (2019), *Security Tokens: A Primer*, Newtown Partners, Cape Town, http://www.newtownpartners.com/wp-content/uploads/2019/01/NTP-Security-Tokens-Primer_FINAL.pdf. [20]

OECD (2019), "Blockchain technologies as a digital enabler for sustainable infrastructure", *OECD Environment Policy Papers*, No. 16, OECD Publishing, Paris, https://dx.doi.org/10.1787/0ec26947-en. [13]

OECD (2018), *Road and Rail Infrastructure in Asia: Investing in Quality*, The Development Dimension, OECD Publishing, Paris, https://dx.doi.org/10.1787/9789264302563-en. [1]

PWC and Urban Land Institute (2018), *Emerging Trends in Real Estate Asia Pacific 201*, Washington D.C., https://www.pwc.com/sg/en/publications/assets/emerging-trends-real-estate-asia-pacific-2019.pdf. [31]

RBI (2019), *Financial Stability Report*, No. 19, June, Reserve Bank of India, Mumbai, https://rbidocs.rbi.org.in/rdocs/PublicationReport/Pdfs/FSRJUNE2019E5ECDDAD7E514756AFEF1E71CB2ADA2B.PDF. [28]

Roth, J., F. Schär and A. Schöpfer (2019), "The Tokenization of Assets: Using Blockchains for Equity Crowdfunding", *SSRN Electronic Journal*, http://dx.doi.org/10.2139/ssrn.3443382. [15]

Simpson, K. (2019), "How tiny Branson, through crowdfunding and new water tech, saved itself from drying up", *The Colorado Sun*, https://coloradosun.com/2019/10/22/branson-water-crowdfunding-success/. [56]

Smart City Embassy (n.d.), *"WeShareSolar – Crowdfunding Solar Energy", webpage*, http://www.smartcityembassy.nl/initiative/wesharesolar/ (accessed on 19 November 2019). [41]

Smith, J. et al. (2019), "Tokenized securities & commercial real estate", *MIT Digital Currency Initiative Working Group Research Paper*, Massachusetts Institute of Technology (MIT) Management Sloane School, Digital Currency Initiative and MIT Media Lab., Cambridge, Massachusetts, https://mitcre.mit.edu/wp-content/uploads/2019/11/Tokenized-Security-Commercial-Real-Estate2.pdf. [27]

Strategy& (2019), *5th ICO/STO Report: A Strategic Perspective*, Strategy&, PricewaterhouseCoopers, New York, http://www.pwc.ch/en/publications/2019/ch-PwC-Strategy&-ICO-Report-Summer-2019.pdf. [11]

Supreme Court of Pakistan (2019), *"Dam Fund Statistics", webpage*, http://www.supremecourt.gov.pk/dam-fund-statistics/ (accessed on 19 November 2019). [57]

The Nation (2019), "Dams Fund receives over Rs 11.32b", The Nation, https://nation.com.pk/26-Oct-2019/dams-fund-receives-over-rs-11-32b. [58]

The Urban Web (2016), "The Luchtsingel pedestrian footbridge in Rotterdam", https://theurbanweb.wordpress.com/2016/11/05/the-luchtsingel-pedestrian-footbridge-in-rotterdam/. [54]

UN ESCAP (2017), *Asia-Pacific Countries with Special Needs Development Report 2017: Investing in Infrastructure for an Inclusive and Sustainable Future*, United Nations Economic and Social Commission for Asia and the Pacific, Bangkok, http://www.unescap.org/sites/default/files/publications/Final%20%28CSN%29%206%20June.pdf. [4]

US SEC (2017), *Report of Investigation Pursuant to Section 21(a) of the Securities Exchange Act of 1934: The DAO, US Securities and Exchange Commission*, Release No. 81207/25 July 2017, http://www.sec.gov/litigation/investreport/34-81207.pdf. [21]

US SEC (2012), *"Municipal Bonds", webpage*, https://www.investor.gov/introduction-investing/general-resources/news-alerts/alerts-bulletins/investor-bulletins/municipal (accessed on 2 March 2020). [46]

Uzsoki, D. (2019), *Tokenization of Infrastructure: A Blockchain-based Solution to Financing Sustainable Infrastructure*, International Institute for Sustainable Development and MAVA Foundation, Winnipeg, http://www.iisd.org/sites/default/files/publications/tokenization-infrastructure-blockchain-solution.pdf. [14]

Wolfson, R. (2018), "A first for Manhattan: $30M real estate property tokenized with blockchain", Forbes, http://www.forbes.com/sites/rachelwolfson/2018/10/03/a-first-for-manhattan-30m-real-estate-property-tokenized-with-blockchain/#25c4cc8c4895. [35]

Yoshino, N., M. Helble and U. Abidhadjaev (eds.) (2018), "Infrastructure investment, private finance and institutional investors: Asia from a global perspective", *Financing Infrastructure in Asia and the Pacific: Capturing Impacts and New Sources*, Asian Development Bank Institute, Tokyo, http://www.adb.org/sites/default/files/publication/394191/adbi-financing-infrastructure-asia-capturing-impacts-and-new-sources.pdf. [6]

Young, K. (2018), "Harbor launches first institutional-grade platform for tokenizing private securities – unlocks access, value and liquidity through blockchain", *Medium*, https://medium.com/harborhq/harbor-launch-and-hub-e76908207680. [37]

Zhao, H. (2018), "Soon you could own shares of this Brooklyn apartment building with tokens costing just a few dollars", *CNBC*, http://www.cnbc.com/2018/03/19/own-shares-of-brooklyn-building-with-tokens-blockchain-real-estate.html. [36]

Ziegler, T. et al. (2019), *"Shifting Paradigms", The 4th European Alternative Finance Benchmarking Report*, University of Cambridge, University of Agderk, Invesco, Cambridge, http://www.jbs.cam.ac.uk/fileadmin/user_upload/research/centres/alternative-finance/downloads/2019-05-4th-european-alternative-finance-benchmarking-industry-report-shifting-paradigms.pdf. [10]

Notes

[1] The Dow Jones Brookfield Asia/Pacific Infrastructure Index, MSCI all-country Asia (excluding Japan) Infrastructure Index, S&P Bombay Stock Exchange India Infrastructure Index, Financial Times Stock Exchange–Infrastructure Development Finance Company Limited India Infrastructure Index, Indxx China Infrastructure Index and Shanghai Stock Exchange Infrastructure Index are examples of listed indices.

[2] Tokenisation replaces sensitive data, such as a credit card number, with a random number to enhance security. Blockchain technology allows for verification without the need for third parties; no single authority has access to data.

3 Inducing private finance to water supply and inland water transport using spillover tax revenues

This chapter assesses the merits of inducing private finance in water supply and inland water transport. It discusses infrastructure investment needs in the region, with particular focus on private participation. It introduces the concept of spillover tax revenues, which are also known as indirect or secondary revenues, or externality effects. The chapter also shows the importance of the spillover effect of water supply and inland water transport on the economy. It then examines financing for water supply through bank loans, insurance funds, pension funds, revenue bonds and equity investment. Finally, it proposes alternatives for financing water supply and inland water transport. This includes returning fractional spillover tax revenues to investors in water projects and offering financing for start-up businesses and small and medium-sized enterprises near the water supply.

Introduction

Water is a necessary public good. While water supply is mostly the domain of the public sector, private investors could help expand the water networks and thus increase the usable water supply. Many countries in the Mekong region lack proper water supply, sanitation and inland water transport. Water supply improvements may create new economic opportunities through spillover effects. Businesses and housing may be attracted to areas that were previously ignored because of the inherent water access difficulties.

Insurance corporations and pension funds are gradually expanding and looking to enlarge their long-term investment portfolios in each country. Public sector funding alone cannot cover the huge demand for infrastructure construction. The engagement of institutional investors such as insurance corporations and pension funds could develop much more infrastructure. Furthermore, private investors could also finance inland water transport, provided that the risk-adjusted rates of return are attractive enough. Nevertheless, high costs and limited returns may be discouraging private sector involvement.

This chapter assesses the merits of inducing private finance in water supply and inland water transport. It discusses infrastructure investment needs in the region, with particular focus on private participation.

Huge needs for infrastructure investment in Asia

Asian countries need different types of infrastructure. Table 3.1 shows the infrastructure investment needed in Asia and the Pacific, as estimated by the Asian Development Bank (2017[1]). The electricity sector has the highest need for infrastructure investment, representing 51.8% of the total, followed by transport, telecommunications, and water and sanitation.

Table 3.1. Infrastructure investment needed in Asia and the Pacific, 2016-30

(USD billion in 2015 prices)

Sector	Baseline estimates		
	Investment	Annual average	Share (%)
Electricity	11 689	779	51.8
Transport (including inland water transport)	7 796	520	34.6
Telecommunications	2 279	152	10.1
Water and sanitation	787	52	3.5
Total	**22 551**	**1 503**	**100**

Source: (Asian Development Bank, 2017[1]).

Spillover effects from water infrastructure investment

Infrastructure investment can boost economic growth

Infrastructure investments increase productivity, in addition to creating massive spillover effects for the economy. Yoshino and Nakahigashi (2004[2]) and Nakahigashi and Yoshino (2016[3]) used macroeconomic data of Japan to estimate the impact of infrastructure investment on the economy. Infrastructure construction, for example, has direct effects by increasing production in key sectors that support construction, among others. Indirect effects, also known as spillover or externality effects, arise from increased production and employment induced by infrastructure investment (Yoshino and Nakahigashi, 2004[2]). As an example of an indirect effect, infrastructure such as water supply will rely on various materials and equipment as inputs. This will in turn lead to job creation in subsectors involved in the manufacturing of these inputs and construction of the project. Infrastructure could also generate a variety of spillover effects. It has the potential to attract private businesses to the region. New retail outlets and factories could be constructed, resulting in higher regional output. This, in turn, will bring employment to the region, increasing consumption and demand for new housing. Improved water supply could prompt the construction of new office buildings and new housing units, which will increase the efficient use of land along the water supply. Water transport could also facilitate tourist and goods flows from neighbouring countries. For instance, the construction of a shopping centre in the port is typically followed by restaurant openings and more hotels could be built in the vicinity of ports, taking advantage of tourists' preference for proximity. All these economic activities could create new jobs in the region.

Table 3.2 provides estimates of the direct effect of infrastructure investment and its spillover effects based on Japanese macro-level data. In 1966-70, the direct effect of infrastructure investment in increasing output was 0.638 (first row). The spillover effect of increasing output induced by growth in private capital was 0.493 (second row), and the spillover effect of increasing output by growth in employment was 0.814 (third row). The biggest spillover effect was increased employment, which contributed to an increase in output (third row). The last row of Table 3.2 presents the share of the total effect of infrastructure investment in Japan from spillover effects. These proportions are quite high at about 66-68%.

Table 3.2. Estimates of spillover effects on increased output in Japan

	1956-60	1961-65	1966-70	1971-75	1976-80	1981-85
Direct effect of infrastructure investment	0.696	0.737	0.638	0.508	0.359	0.275
Spillover effect through private capital (Kp)	0.452	0.557	0.493	0.389	0.270	0.203
Spillover effect through employment (L)	1.071	0.973	0.814	0.639	0.448	0.350
Spillover effects of infrastructure investment (percentage)	68.644	67.481	67.210	66.907	66.691	66.777
	1986-90	**1991-95**	**1996-2000**	**2001-05**	**2006-10**	
Direct effect of infrastructure investment	0.215	0.181	0.135	0.114	0.108	
Spillover effect through private capital (Kp)	0.174	0.146	0.110	0.091	0.085	
Spillover effect through employment (L)	0.247	0.208	0.154	0.132	0.125	
Spillover effects of infrastructure investment (percentage)	66.222	66.200	66.094	66.122	66.139	

Source: (Nakahigashi and Yoshino, 2016[3]).

Figure 3.1 illustrates the spillover effects of the water supply. The red diagonal line represents the water supply and new water supply to be constructed. Along these water supply corridors, new industries and companies could come into the region to set up manufacturing activities. Apartments for housing are likely to be constructed along the new water supply routes, followed by restaurants and other service sector establishments. Hence, the yellow part of Figure 3.1 depicts the spillover effects created by the new water supply.

This economic development will have positive effects on regional output. This, in turn, will lead to an increase in both local and central government tax revenues. Past experience has shown, however, that all these incremental tax revenues mainly benefitted local and central governments rather than being returned to water supply companies that relied solely on user charges as source of returns. This state of things has been deterring many private investors from investing in water supply projects. Water supply thus relied on public money, which restricted expansion in many parts of developing Asia. The rate of return from the water supply would increase if spillover tax revenues were partly returned to private investors. This, in turn, would encourage private investors such as insurance corporations and pension funds together with banks to invest in water supply, which could expand the water supply network.

Figure 3.1. Spillover effects of water supply

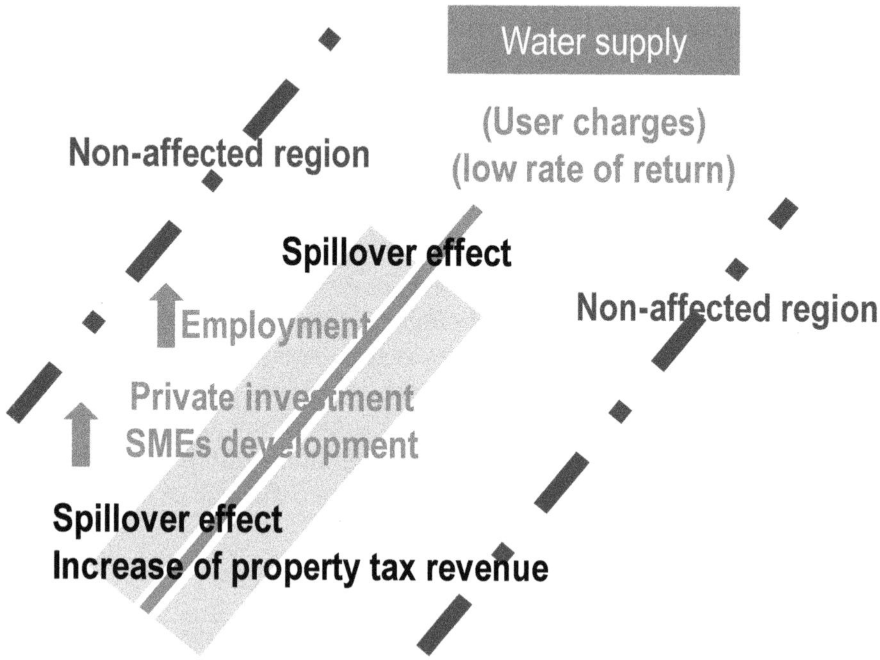

Note: SMEs = small and medium-sized enterprises.
Source: Authors.

Estimates of spillover effects of infrastructure investment on connectivity

This section estimates spillover effects of three cases of infrastructure investment in Asian countries: the railway in Uzbekistan, the high-speed railway on Kyushu Island in Japan and the expressway in Manila (Yoshino and Pontines, 2018[4]). It defines a dummy variable for before and after the construction periods by taking the difference in the tax revenues between two regions. Specifically, it takes a value of 1 for the region along the infrastructure and 0 for other regions where there was no impact from the infrastructure investment.

As shown in Table 3.3, the economy along the railway in Uzbekistan grew by 2 percentage points more than in other regions. This difference was due to the spillover effects after the railway connected the production region to the market, which generated additional tax revenues for the government (Yoshino and Abidhadjaev, 2017[5]).

Table 3.3. Estimated difference in gross domestic product before and after railway construction in Uzbekistan

Region group	Outcome	Pre-railway period 2005-08	Post-railway period 2009-12	Difference (percentage points)
Non-affected group	Average GDP growth rate (percentage)	8.3	8.5	0.2
Affected group	Average GDP growth rate (percentage)	7.2	9.4	2.2
		Difference	**2.0**	

Note: GDP = gross domestic product. Affected group includes the regions of Samarkand, Surkandharya, Tashkent and the Republic of Karakalpakstan.
Source: (Yoshino and Abidhadjaev, 2017[5]).

This difference-in-difference approach represents the effect of the treatment, which in this case is the railway project in Uzbekistan.

Table 3.4 shows the case of the Star Highway in Manila (Yoshino and Pontines, 2018[4]). The periods $t-1$ and t indicate periods under construction. At the end of t, the highway had been completed and started operation. For Batangas City (last row), tax revenues increased from nearly PHP 491 billion without construction ($t-2$) to over PHP 622 billion (Philippine peso) and PHP 652 billion after construction had started ($t-1$ and t).

During the highway construction, construction workers and related construction projects came to the region, which increased regional GDP. At the end of t, the Star Highway had been completed. Then, at $t+2$, tax revenues diminished compared with the construction period until after the fourth year when tax revenues increased drastically. At $t+4$, tax revenues reached PHP 1 208 billion, about twice as much as before the construction. These are the spillover tax increases coming from infrastructure investment, in this case the Star Highway.

These tax revenues are the increases, not the existing tax revenue. Due to the highway construction and increased economic activities, Batangas City had gained tax revenues of PHP 1 208 billion by $t+4$ because of the highway construction and increased economic activities. If part of these incremental tax revenues (PHP 1 209 billion–PHP 490 billion) were to be returned to private investors, it is highly likely that they would be willing to invest in the construction of the highway. The same effects apply to the construction of new water supply infrastructure.

Table 3.4. Calculated increase in business tax revenues for the beneficiary group relative to non-beneficiary group

(PHP million)

Region	$t-2$	$t-1$	t	$t+1$	$t+2$	$t+3$	$t+4$
Lipa City	134.36	173.50	249.70	184.47	191.81	257.35	371.93
Ibaan City	5.84	7.04	7.97	6.80	5.46	10.05	12.94
Batangas City	490.90	622.65	652.83	637.83	599.49	742.28	1 209.61

Source: (Yoshino and Pontines, 2018[4]).

In the case of the high-speed railway of Kyushu Railway Company (JR Kyushu) in Japan (Yoshino and Abidhadjaev, 2017[6]), the study compared tax revenues in three periods: (i) the construction period; (ii) the operational period without good connectivity; and (iii) the operational period with good connectivity to large cities such as Osaka and Tokyo. It also compared total tax revenues, as well as revenues from personal income tax, corporate tax and other taxes (including property tax), for the three different periods (Figure 3.2). When construction started, speculators who anticipated a significant rise of property values started buying land along the high-speed railway. This caused property tax revenues to increase significantly (denoted in Figure 3.2 as "other taxes"). The project involved hiring many workers and construction companies in the region, which increased revenue from both personal and corporate taxes. Due to the operational period when there was no connectivity with large cities such as Osaka and Tokyo, revenues from personal income tax and corporate tax decreased in the short term compared to the construction period. Eventually, connectivity with Osaka and Tokyo brought businesses and passengers into the region, which created a dramatic increase in corporate and individual income taxes associated with local economic expansion. Furthermore, the expectation of continued increases in the value of property proximal to the railway increased property tax revenue, as is shown in "other taxes" revenues in Figure 3.2.

Figure 3.2. Changes in tax revenues by connectivity in high-speed railway

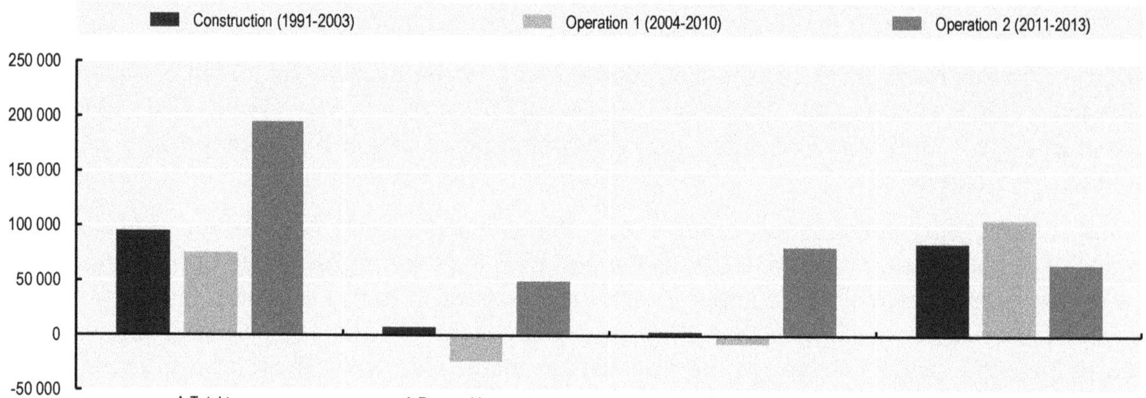

	Δ Total tax	Δ Personal income tax	Δ Corporate tax	Δ Other taxes
Construction (1991-2003)	94 896	7 447	3 435	84 012
Operation 1 (2004-2010)	75 131	-23 843	-6 883	105 858
Operation 2 (2011-2013)	194 790	49 860	80 998	65 102

StatLink https://doi.org/10.1787/888934167619

Source: (Yoshino and Abidhadjaev, 2017[6]).

The spillover effects can be ascertained through the following procedure, presented diagrammatically in Figure 3.3:

1. Compute the national average growth rate of tax revenues in each tax category, such as corporate tax, personal income tax, property tax, sales tax, etc.
2. Compute the growth rate of all tax revenues along the newly constructed infrastructure, such as roads, highways, railways, water supply, etc.
3. Take the difference between (1) and (2) by defining the difference as spillover effects.

Figure 3.3. Spillover tax revenues of affected region vs. national average tax revenues

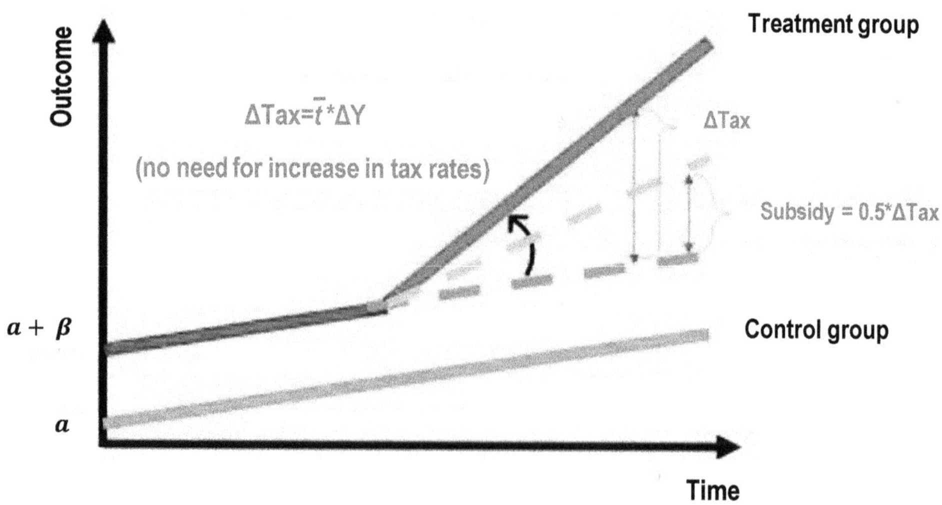

Source: Authors.

Without investment in infrastructure, the government would not obtain the increased tax revenues. Part of the tax revenues could be distributed to private investors who financed the infrastructure without decreasing existing tax revenues of local and central governments. The proposed method of returning spillover tax revenues to investors would encourage the development of rural regions. In the Philippines, the central government finances much of the infrastructure development. However, local governments collect most of the spillover tax revenues, which increases their tax revenues. If local governments return a part of their increased spillover tax revenues to the central government, the central government can invest those returned tax revenues into other projects to help mitigate poverty in rural regions. These projects would generate additional tax revenues from spillovers and so on. The proposed return of the spillover tax revenues to private investors also applies to central governments as appropriate.

Economic impact of inland water transport

Inland water transport is a high priority in the Mekong region, but the development of ports and other facilities has not advanced well. Ministries that manage inland water transport receive most of their revenue from user charges paid by owners of boats and ships. Governments have not given enough consideration to the regional development of inland water transport; yet ports can become tourist attractions to create employment in the region and greatly expand markets for farmers to sell their produce. Spillover tax revenues will be created when the inland water transport brings businesses into the region and local and central governments can earn much higher tax revenues from property tax, corporate tax, income tax and sales tax than from user charges collected from boats and ships.

Figure 3.4 graphically illustrates the mechanisms through which spillover effects reduce user charges and increase the rate of return from inland water transport. The red curve represents the total hypothetical gains in terms of tax revenues. If a portion of the additional tax revenues were returned to private investors, the investors' rate of return from inland water transport would shift from the green line (user charges only) to the blue dotted curve. The difference between the green line and the blue line therefore illustrates the additional returns for private investors after transfer. Increased inland waterway transport could have significant business and employment effects, while the incremental tax revenues would expand even more as a result of more economic dynamism. In other words, government revenues would benefit from additional revenue sources.

Figure 3.4. Injection of increased tax revenues to increase rate of return

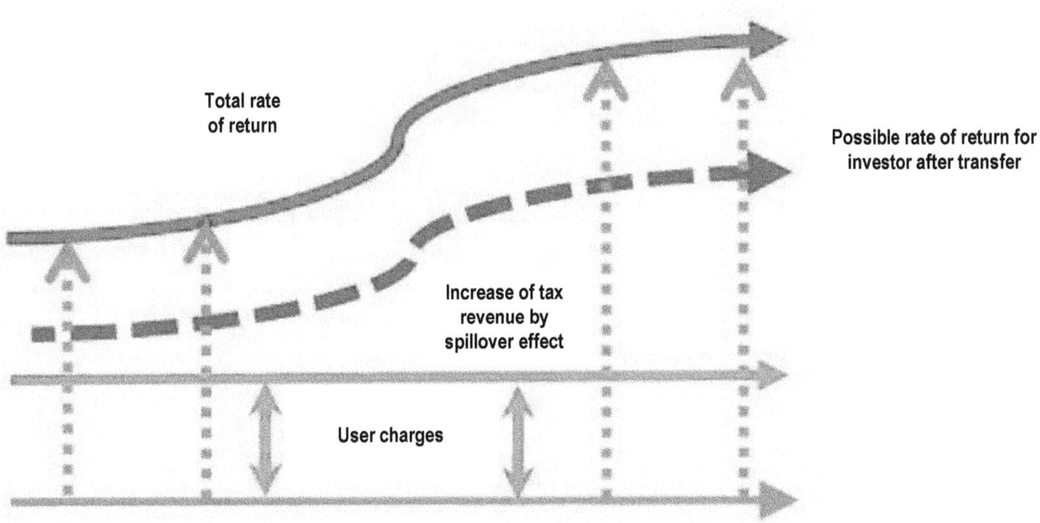

Source: Authors.

Water supply and inland water transport will be able to create a bigger economic impact in regions with larger population densities. However, rural regions may not be able to create such sizeable spillover effects and the incremental tax revenues might not be large. The government can set up a cap for private investors. A cap of 15%, for example, means that if the total rate of return (part of spillover tax revenues and user charges) surpasses 15%, the government would take the yellow portion of increased tax revenues (Figure 3.5). It would then use the extra tax revenues to supply water to less densely populated rural regions. This would mitigate urban and rural mismatches of water supply.

Figure 3.5. Injection of increased tax revenues to increase rate of return with government cap

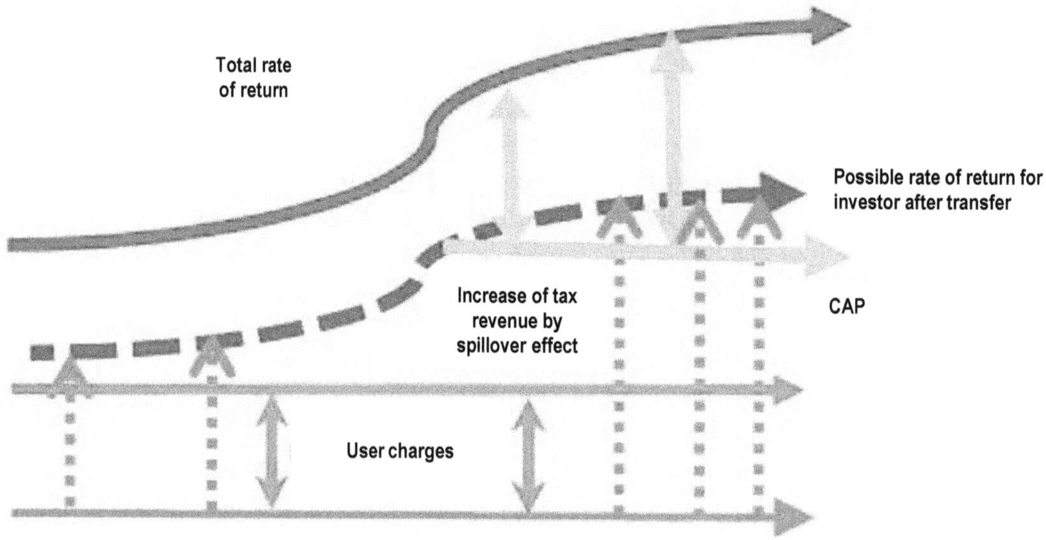

Source: Authors.

Financing for water supply and inland water transport

There are five different methods of private finance for water supply and inland water transport (Figure 3.6): (i) bank loans; (ii) insurance corporations; (iii) pension funds; (iv) revenue bonds; and (v) equity investment. Bank loans have relatively short tenors (one to five years), insurance corporations typically have a medium tenor (10 to 20 years), while pension funds have much longer investment horizons. The next three subsections provide an overview of these three financing methods.

Pension funds

In the coming years, many Asian countries will be faced with ageing populations. Public pension funds must be well-established, and private insurance systems must be ready to cope with this change in demographics. Once collection begins for insurance and pension funds, these long-term assets must be matched by long-term investment opportunities. For instance, insurance is growing in Thailand as a source of finance for this purpose. Water supply and inland water transport needs in the Asian region are large in scale and cost, requiring enormous funding for infrastructure construction.

Figure 3.6. Different classes of infrastructure assets and types of finance

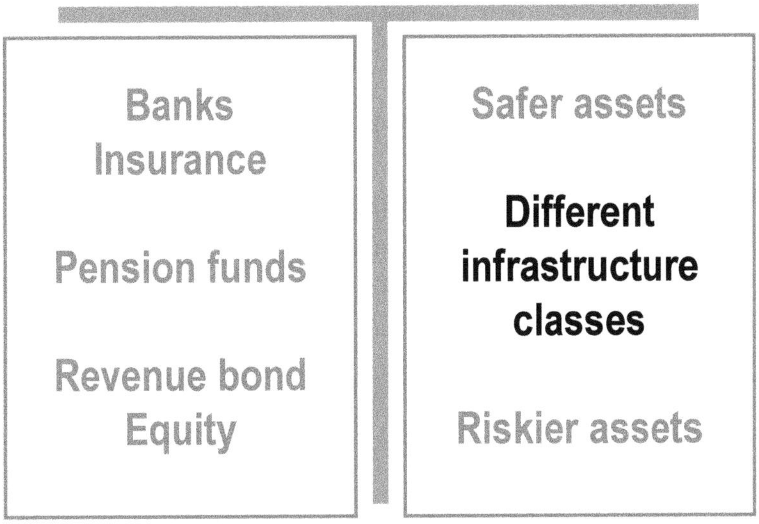

Source: Authors.

The right-hand side of Figure 3.6 shows safer infrastructure assets at the top and riskier infrastructure assets at the bottom. There are many different kinds of asset classes in water supply investment. Safe assets may be represented by water supply in large cities and densely populated urban regions. The private sector can expect continuous revenues from existing water supply operations. If the rate of return from the existing water supply is high, private investors can invest in brownfield infrastructure, which represents a relatively safe asset. At the bottom are risky infrastructure assets, such as water supply in new towns and rural regions; it is unclear how much revenue these assets could create. If spillover tax revenues from water supply are returned to investors, as proposed, the rate of return for private investors would increase significantly. Even risky infrastructure assets can be deemed worthwhile investments if the extra spillover tax revenues created in large cities are injected. Thus, the rate of return for all kinds of water supply investment can be increased. Similarly, the safe assets in infrastructure investment could be increased, thereby providing insurance corporations and pension funds with an incentive to invest in domestic water supply.

Revenue bonds

If the water supply agency, which captures not only the user charges but also part of the spillover tax revenues, earns sufficient annual revenue (Figure 3.7), it can issue revenue bonds. The interest rate on revenue bonds changes based on the revenues created by the user charges and spillover tax revenues. If business is strong, the spillover tax revenues will rise, and the revenue bond will achieve a higher rate of return, reflected in a higher interest rate. Revenue bonds can be purchased by a mix of entities. As an example, these could comprise the central government (20%), private investors (40%) and local government (40%). The entities share all the risks but also the benefits, each in proportion to their investment. The exact proportions would need to be negotiated for each project, the distribution suggested previously above being for illustrative purposes only.

Figure 3.7. Revenue bond for water supply

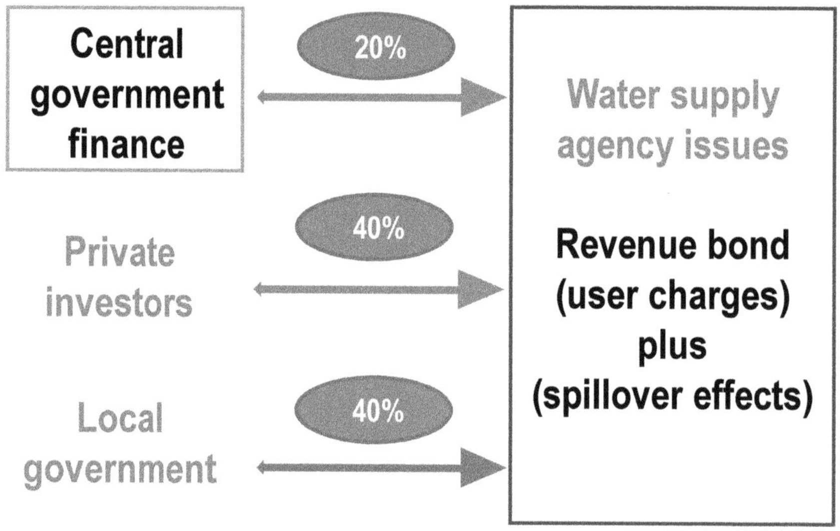

Source: Authors.

Bond and equity investment

Figure 3.8 illustrates equity and bond investment in water supply. The right-hand side shows that the water supply company raises funds by issuing bonds and equity. User charges and spillover effects are both returned to equity and bondholders. Such a mix, for example, might include 20% from the Asian Development Bank, 50% from fixed interest rate bonds and 30% from the stock market. If spillover tax revenues are returned to water supply investment investors, the rate of return of this fixed bond would be significantly higher. If the rate of return from user charges and spillover tax revenues were much higher than expected, then equity investors in the bottom 30% would also enjoy excess benefits.

Figure 3.8. Equity and bond investment for water supply

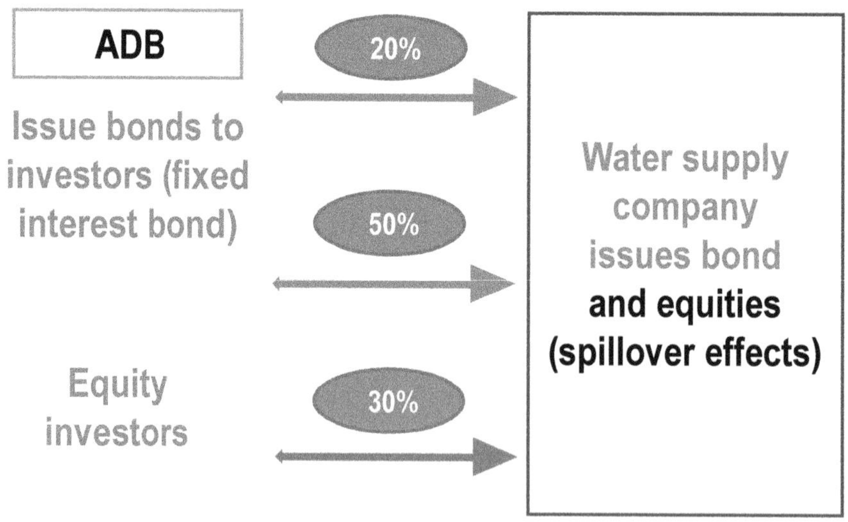

Note: ADB = Asian Development Bank.
Source: Authors.

However, various risks are also associated with water supply investment, including but not limited to:

- Political risk
- Construction risk
- Operation and maintenance risk
- Exchange rate risk, if the investors are from overseas
- Environmental risk (often associated with infrastructure investment).

Addressing the mechanisms for dealing with each of these risks lies beyond the scope of this publication.

Models for returning fractional spillover tax revenues to investors in water projects

It is especially difficult to induce private-sector financing in water supply. User charges are kept low, and the rate of return from these charges is not expected to cover the construction and other costs. Spillover tax revenues must be returned to investors in this case or water shortages are likely to continue. If the rate of return is increased, as explained earlier, private investors may be willing to invest in construction and other up-front costs.

Spillover tax revenues created by the water supply could be used. The United States, for example, has used property tax revenues to increase the rate of return to infrastructure investors. This study suggests using not only property tax revenues, but also revenue from a variety of other taxes. These revenues would be returned to water supply investors. Increased spillover tax revenues should be shared with the local government and private investors in infrastructure investment.

The development of territories proximal to water supplies and inland water transport would not create service monopolies. Issuance of infrastructure bonds and their wide dissemination in the market will distribute ownership. At the same time, the water supply infrastructure firm will diversify its revenue streams by promoting secondary activities such as real estate. The revenue streams from these secondary activities may be more or less volatile than those from the main project. Subsequently, water tariffs and fares will decline, making households better off. This will have an impact on the local economy and raise the marginal productivity of capital. This, in turn, will increase tax revenues, assuming the tax rates are held constant. Returning part of this net increase in tax revenue to the water supply firm will push utility fees further down and make households better off still. This will increase the viability of a water supply project and contribute to the sustainable development of the region.

Return of spillover tax revenues

Figure 3.9 shows a model for the return of spillover tax revenues to private investors. The bottom rectangle illustrates the increased tax revenues created by spillover effects of the water supply. The government could subsequently inject a portion of these spillover revenues as subsidies to private investors.

Figure 3.9. Injection of fraction of tax revenues as subsidy

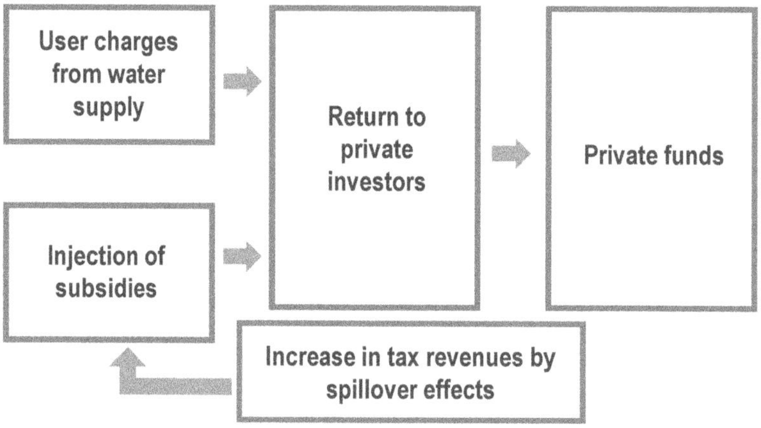

Source: Authors.

Financing for start-up businesses and small and medium-sized enterprises along water supply

Financing could also be available for start-up businesses together with the new water supply. If clean water is supplied in a new region, many entrepreneurs will be interested in starting a business because new residents will be available as customers. However, start-up businesses often find it difficult to raise initial capital, and banks' tight lending standards often deprive them of bank loans. About 20 years ago, Japan created hometown investment trust funds, a concept that expanded to Cambodia, Viet Nam and Peru. In such instances of hometown crowdfunding, money is collected from individuals in the region. When the water supply becomes operational, many people in the region contribute small amounts of money to local business entrepreneurs that would otherwise be unavailable through the bank lending channel.

While water supply is important to regional development, financing for small businesses along with a new water supply will mitigate income inequality and create business opportunities for start-ups. The approach will increase spillover effects from water supply by allowing new businesses to start in the region. Hometown crowdfunding can thus finance both the water supply and new business development within the water supply region in turn. This will increase the spillover effects and the number of interested investors, the average size of investment, or both.

However, tax collection in many developing countries is difficult. Small and medium-sized enterprises do not pay tax, and even large businesses hide their revenue. To counter this practice, the Philippine Finance Minister and Asian Development Bank Dean have suggested using satellite data for proper tax collection. These data could help identify how many people come to shopping malls or restaurants every day, how long the opening hours are, how many trucks deliver to each factory, how much greenery a farmland contains and so on. Satellite data can provide tax authorities with rough figures of business activities and even estimates of farm crops. Such satellite data could capture spillover tax revenues properly and thus increase the rate of return to investors in water supply. However, incentivising both households and businesses to shift from cash to digital payments may be an easier path. In either case; improved digital infrastructure, digital literacy and cyber security will be essential precursors of implementation.

Various infrastructure projects and the allocation of spillover tax revenues

In many cases, various infrastructure investments, such as electricity, water supply, roads, etc., are constructed simultaneously. Estimates in previous sections focused on the use of one infrastructure project such as high-speed rail; none referred to infrastructure investments of, for example, electricity, water supply and port re-development occurring simultaneously.

Inland water transport will bring tourists and commodities from various regions to the port. A large distribution of goods and visitors from various parts of the river will make the port a focal point for business and tourism. Inland water services, as well as electricity and water supply, must be provided to develop the river basin region. If various infrastructure investment comes together, spillover tax revenues must be allocated among parties.

There will be two ways to identify the impact on spillover tax revenues created by each infrastructure investment.

- **Staggered infrastructure projects**. In this scenario, the use of annual dummy variables can identify spillover effects for each type of investment project (Figure 3.10, Panel A.). First, for example, electricity is supplied at point b. An increase in tax revenues follows. A few months later, in period c, the water supply is completed. An additional increase in various tax revenues will arise. Then the inland water facility at the port will be renewed. Point d observes a further increase in tax revenues. Spillover tax revenues will be different in each period (b, c, d). This will allow for the identification of different economic impacts in the region. This, in turn, will allow for spillover tax revenues to be allocated to different kinds of infrastructure investments.
- **Simultaneous infrastructure projects**. In this scenario, it is difficult to measure the impact of tax revenues created by each infrastructure project separately as shown in Figure 3.10, Panel A. Many different kinds of spillover effects can be computed one by one. They derive from different kinds of infrastructure investments such as electricity, water supply, inland water, road, etc. Each individual impact on spillover tax revenues may not be easily distinguishable from the spillover impact of past infrastructure investments. Panel B and Panel C in Figure 3.10 provide a comparison of spillover tax revenues for water supply and electricity.

Figure 3.10. Subsidy based on additional flow of tax revenue due to various infrastructure investments

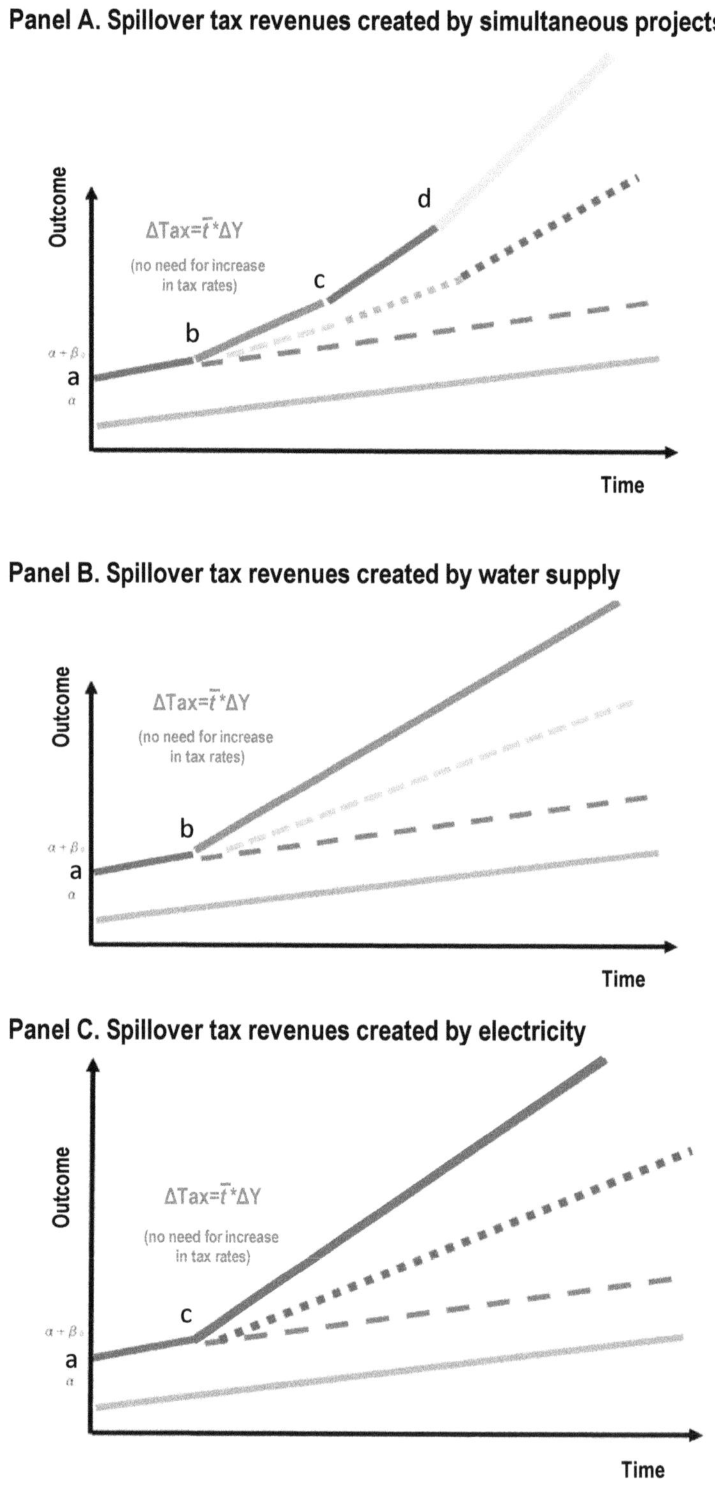

Source: Authors.

Conclusion

Water supplies are essential public goods and there are huge infrastructure needs in the Mekong region, in particular. This chapter discusses the importance of the spillover effect of water supply and inland water transport on the economy by using the concept of spillover tax revenues, which are also known as indirect or secondary revenues. The engagement of private investors needs to be further strengthened and appropriate setting of the risk-adjusted rates of return is critical to encourage private sector participation.

References

Asian Development Bank (2017), *Meeting Asia's Infrastructure Needs*, Asian Development Bank, Manila, Philippines, http://dx.doi.org/10.22617/fls168388-2. [1]

Nakahigashi, M. and N. Yoshino (2016), "Changes in economic effect of infrastructure and method", *Public Policy Review*, Vol. 12/1, Policy Research Institute, Tokyo, pp. 47-68. [3]

Yoshino, N. and U. Abidhadjaev (2017), "An impact evaluation of investment in infrastructure: The case of a railway connection in Uzbekistan", *Journal of Asian Economics*, Vol. 49/April, Elsevier, Amsterdam, pp. 1-11, https://www.adb.org/sites/default/files/publication/175724/adbi-wp548.pdf. [5]

Yoshino, N. and U. Abidhadjaev (2017), "Impact of infrastructure on tax revenue: Case study of high-speed train in Japan", *Journal of Infrastructure, Policy and Development*, Vol. 1/2, Enpress Publisher LLC, Tustin, US, pp. 129-48. [6]

Yoshino, N. and M. Nakahigashi (2004), "The role of infrastructure in economic development", *The ICFAI Journal of Managerial Economics*, Vol. 2, Hyderabad E.N. Murthy, pp. 7-24. [2]

Yoshino, N. and V. Pontines (2018), "The highway effect on public finance: Case of the STAR highway in the Philippines", *Financing Infrastructure in Asia and the Pacific: Capturing Impacts and New Sources*, Asian Development Bank Institute, Tokyo, https://www.adb.org/publications/highway-effect-public-finance-case-star-highway-philippines. [4]

4 Water infrastructure resilient to natural disasters and COVID-19

Countries in the Mekong region are particularly prone to natural disasters such as floods, storms, drought, earthquakes, landslides and epidemics. Climate change, rapid and unplanned urbanisation, as well as environmental degradation, are among factors that increase countries' vulnerability to natural hazards. Since these external shocks can threaten livelihoods, destroy infrastructure or other physical capital and lead to significant socio-economic consequences, improving resilience against natural disasters is essential. The COVID-19 pandemic has also demonstrated the need to build resilience against shocks to curb the infection rate and minimise damage. This chapter discusses the role of resilient water infrastructure, community engagement and the use of digital tools in strengthening preparedness against natural disasters. It also addresses water-related challenges and several preparedness and response initiatives during the pandemic.

Introduction

Natural disasters can slow development by destroying infrastructure and other forms of physical capital (OECD, 2019[1]). Loss of life, population displacement and interruption in economic activity are inevitable when the magnitude of disaster is large enough to threaten livelihoods. The impact of natural disasters on water infrastructure can drive communities back into difficulties. Damage to water infrastructure stemming from natural hazards may contaminate water and disrupt service provision, leaving communities with unsafe and unreliable water supplies. Besides the socio-economic impact, lack of water supply can increase exposure of communities to water-borne disease. This threat is particularly significant during flood events.

Risk of exposure to natural disasters may increase due to climate change, rapid population growth and urbanisation, and environmental degradation (ASEAN, 2017[2]). For instance, climate change is likely increasing the variability of rainfall patterns and intensity, which may bring serious consequences such as floods and drought. Moreover, higher water temperatures could also reduce the self-purifying capacity of freshwater bodies, thereby increasing the risks of water pollution and pathogenic contamination (UNESCO, UN-WATER, 2020[3]).

This chapter discusses several policy responses to cope with natural disasters, beginning with an overview of natural disasters in Mekong countries. It then explores how multi-purpose infrastructure, including nature-based solutions, may help improve resilience against natural hazards while offering other benefits. Next, it focuses on challenges faced by the Mekong region with regard to community-based disaster risk management and the use of digital tools for early warning. Finally, the chapter examines how water infrastructure became crucial during the recent COVID-19 outbreak and how water infrastructure problems affect the most vulnerable populations living in disaster-prone areas.

Overview of natural disasters in Mekong countries

Located in one of the most disaster-prone regions in the world, Mekong countries are particularly vulnerable to water-related disasters. Hydro-meteorological hazards such as floods and storms are the most frequent events. In all, 86 floods and 46 storms were recorded over the last decade. Among the five countries, Viet Nam had the highest exposure to these events, with 33 floods and 31 storms occurring over the same period (Figure 4.1). Drought, earthquakes, landslides and epidemics are also common in Mekong countries. In Thailand, drought and storms occur with the same frequency, while landslides are a major concern in Myanmar.

Figure 4.1. Occurrences of natural disasters in Mekong countries, by country, 2010-20

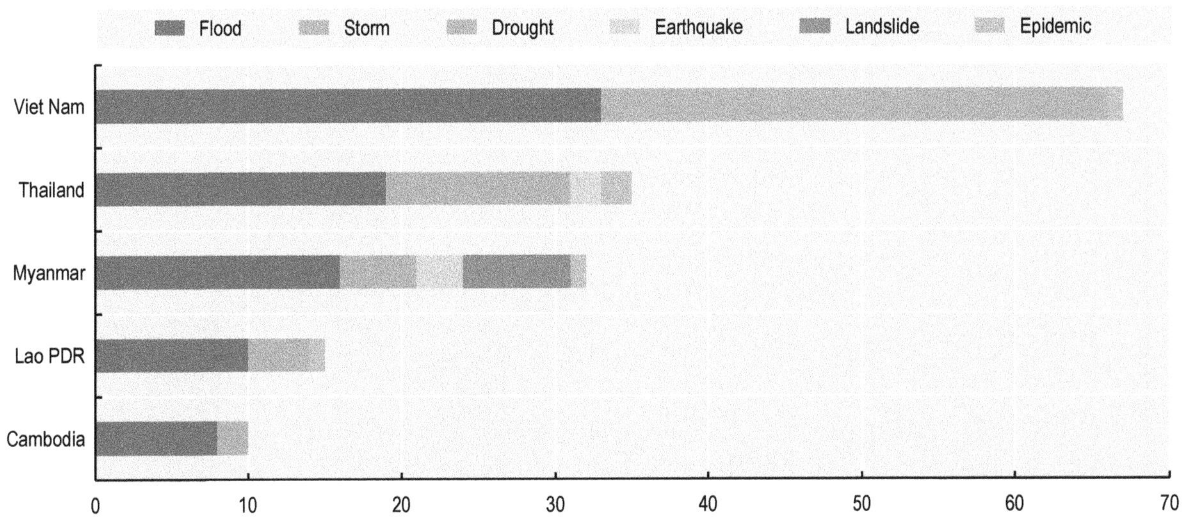

StatLink https://doi.org/10.1787/888934167638

Note: Flood includes flash flood and riverine flood; storm includes convective storm and tropical cyclone; and epidemic includes viral diseases such as dengue and measles.
Source: (CRED, 2020[4]), *Emergency Events Database* (database), www.emdat.be/.

Droughts, flash floods, riverine floods and tropical cyclones occurred more frequently than other natural hazards in Mekong countries. Flash floods may happen during a short heavy rainfall or thunderstorm, while riverine flood occurs when a river exceeds its capacity due to excessive rainfall for a relatively long period. Among the four types of water-related disasters, riverine floods occur most frequently and have caused the most damage. Despite their frequency, tropical cyclones have caused relatively little damage (Figure 4.2).

Over the last decade, riverine floods have been the most damaging water-related disasters in Cambodia, Myanmar and Thailand. Riverine floods affected Cambodia in 2011, Myanmar in 2015 and Thailand in 2011. Total estimated damages were USD 521 million (4.1% of gross domestic product, GDP), USD 119 million (0.2% of GDP) and USD 40 billion (10.8% of GDP), respectively (CRED, 2020[4]). In Lao PDR, the most damaging event over the last decade was a tropical cyclone in 2018. Estimated total damage from the event totalled USD 225 million (1.3% of GDP). Drought may also become a serious concern for Mekong countries. It occurs relatively infrequently, but, when it does occur, the damage is typically high (Figure 4.2). For instance, the Viet Nam drought in 2015 caused an estimated USD 6.75 billion in damage, representing 3.5% of GDP. This represented the most damage from a water-related disaster in the country. Thailand is the most drought-prone in the region and it suffered a loss of USD 3.3 billion (0.8% of GDP) from the 2015 drought.

Figure 4.2. Water-related disasters in Mekong countries, 2010-20

Occurrences and damages

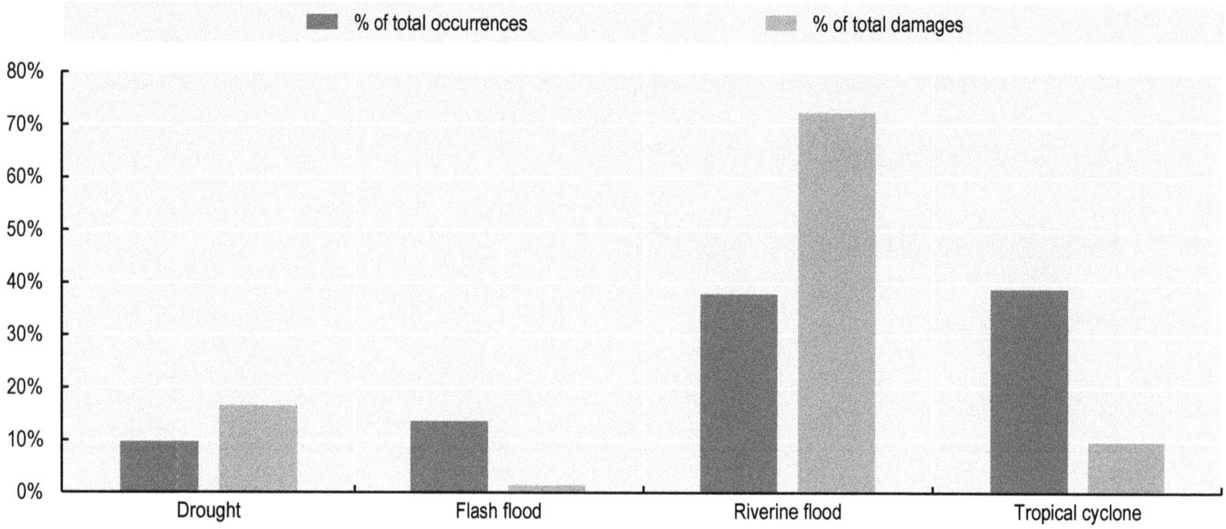

StatLink https://doi.org/10.1787/888934167657

Note: The Mekong countries refer to Cambodia, Lao PDR, Myanmar, Thailand and Viet Nam.
Source: (CRED, 2020[4]), *Emergency Events Database* (database), www.emdat.be/.

The high degree of loss from a disaster may depend on either the magnitude of the disaster itself, capacity to mitigate the impact, or both. Improving water infrastructure towards more disaster resilience, especially against riverine flood and drought, may help Mekong countries minimise damages from water-related hazards.

Adapting to natural disasters with multi-purpose water infrastructure

With the increasing risk of exposure to natural disasters, conventional water infrastructure is growing more vulnerable to natural hazards. This type of infrastructure is often single-purpose and might have limited capacity to mitigate disasters. It may also incur increasingly high costs or adverse societal and environmental impacts (UNESCO, UN-WATER, 2020[3]). Conversely, multi-purpose water infrastructure projects may help meet the challenges of rising vulnerability. This type of infrastructure refers to any type of constructed water system intended to serve more than one purpose for economic, social and environmental activities (Table 4.1). This could include dams, dykes, reservoirs, irrigation canals and water supply networks. For instance, while storing water during the dry period is often a dam's main function, its capacity can be increased to cope with floods during the wet season (UNESCO, UN-WATER, 2020[3]).

Table 4.1. Multi-purpose water infrastructure

Application	Definition
Hydropower generation	When combined with a hydropower plant, dams can generate hydroelectric power.
Irrigation for agriculture	Water stored in a reservoir can irrigate agricultural crops, typically through a network of distribution canals.
Drinking water supply	Reservoir storage capacities and water distribution networks can be used to supply drinking water for human consumption.
Water supply for industrial needs	Water storage can also be used for industry, including power plants for electricity generation.
Transport and navigation	Multi-purpose water systems such as canals and regulation of surface water by dams can provide navigation and transport services.
Flood control	Dam structures and reservoirs may offer flood protection by regulating water discharge and balancing runoff differences.
Strategic water storage	Multi-purpose water infrastructures are also used to mitigate the effects of climate variability and provide a strategic water "buffer", which may be used for some of the above purposes.

Source: (ICOLD, 2014[5]), *International Commission on Large Dams website*, www.icold-cigb.org; (OECD, 2017[6]), *Multi-Purpose Water Infrastructure: Recommendations to maximise economic benefits*, OECD Policy Perspectives, OECD, Paris.

About 30% of large dams globally are considered to be designed as multi-purpose (OECD, 2017[6]), but they are far less common in the Mekong basin countries. Multi-purpose dams account for only 1% of total dams in Cambodia, Lao PDR, Thailand and Viet Nam (Figure 4.3). Most dams are built for hydropower or irrigation. This is particularly the case in Lao PDR, where 96% of dams are for hydropower, and Thailand, where 95% of dams are for irrigation (Figure 4.3).

Single-purpose dams are often more financially attractive for private investors, particularly for hydropower, as they have lower risks and secure financial returns on the energy produced. Conversely, financing for multi-purpose dams often comes from public resources as attracting private investors remains challenging. Multi-purpose dams require capacity to deal with multiple stakeholders. They also need sustainable business models for financing, including operation and maintenance, and contingency for risks and negative externalities (OECD, 2017[6]). In practice, many single-purpose water infrastructures have evolved into multi-purpose ones. However, when dams are designed to be multi-purpose from inception, they may optimise the economic benefits.

Figure 4.3. Dams in the Mekong basin by type and by country, 2017

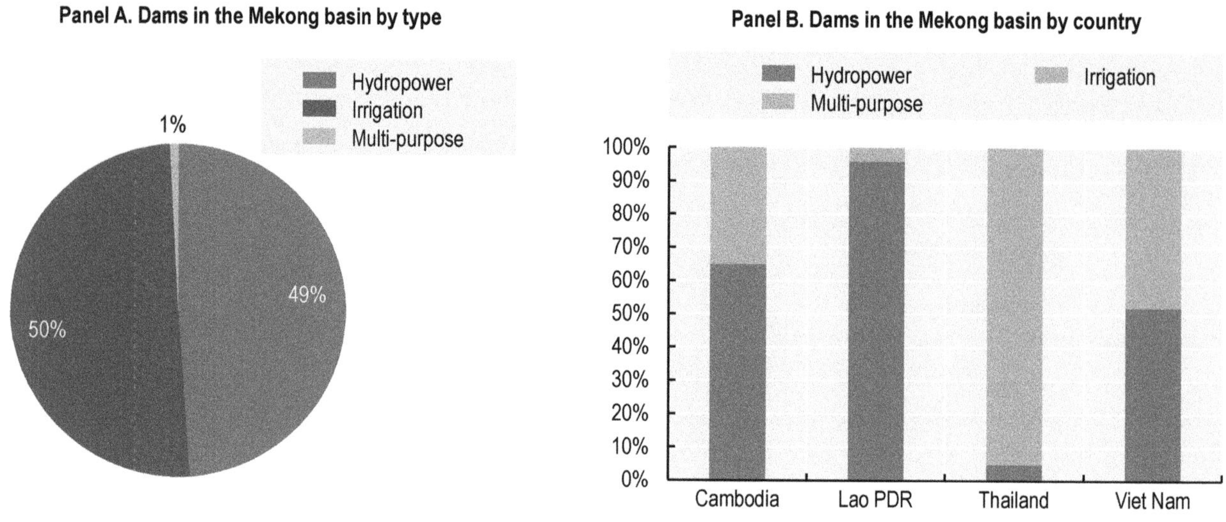

StatLink https://doi.org/10.1787/888934167676

Note: All dams include commissioned, under construction and planned dams in parts of the Mekong river basin in Cambodia, Lao PDR, Thailand and Viet Nam. Only hydropower dams of 15 megawatts installed capacity and above are indicated; only irrigation reservoirs of 0.5 km^2 and above are indicated.
Source: (WLE Greater Mekong, 2018[7]), *CGIAR Research Program on Water, Land and Ecosystems – Greater Mekong*.

Another challenge related to resilient water infrastructure development in the Mekong region is the lack of joint planning between border provinces (MRC, 2017[8]). Infrastructure development in one country can aim to lower the impact of disaster, but it can also have unintended transboundary effects. Infrastructure projects often affect water flow, contributing to flooding or drought in the neighbouring country. In the Mekong delta region, for instance, the development of a canal system for flood control and irrigation in Viet Nam increases water levels in Cambodia during the flood period. For its part, infrastructure development in the Cambodian floodplain has affected Viet Nam through changes in hydrological regimes and flood characteristics of the delta. This highlights the need for strategic planning that addresses transboundary issues between countries and improves infrastructure development. Such development is limited to national interests, and needs to properly account for its cross-border impacts.

Strengthening urban resilience with nature-based solutions

Nature-based solutions (NBS) encompass interventions in ecosystems inspired and supported by nature. They have often been considered to complement, or even substitute, grey or conventional infrastructure. This concept may offer effective and low-cost solutions to increase resilience, while delivering other benefits such as biodiversity, air quality or even recreation. Examples of NBS include forest restoration to improve soil quality and biodiversity, or mangrove reforestation to reduce the impact of waves, storm surges and coastal erosion. NBS can also help achieve water-related objectives, such as wetlands restoration for improving water resources management and boosting resilience against water-related hazards.

Within the urban landscape, NBS includes water-sensitive urban design (WSUD). This integrates water flows into urban landscaping and considers all aspects of the urban water cycle as a valuable resource (ADB, 2019[9]). WSUD tools include vegetated swales, cleansing biotopes, wetlands, rain gardens and green roofs, among others. WSUD is a relatively new approach in developing Asian cities, especially in the Mekong region. However, the concept may gain importance as cities become more vulnerable to climate change-induced disasters and environmental degradation. Fast-growing urbanisation has often disrupted natural urban drainage, leading to increased risk of flooding, waterlogging and water quality degradation. As important drivers of economic performance, cities must face these challenges by improving their resilience or suffer significant socio-economic consequences. WSUD tools can be easily integrated into any type of urban development, such as building units, parks and other open spaces with waterways. The concept may thus offer solutions for cities to become more resilient and liveable, while providing vibrant spaces for community by attracting people closer to water.

The application of WSUD in Mekong countries is limited and still at an early stage. An example of initiative is the proposal for Go Vap Cultural Park in Ho Chi Minh City to be developed as an attractive river park for the community, as well as a floodplain park that could help lower flood levels during storm events (ADB, 2019[9]). Other initiatives are the Sen Pond in Hue City, Viet Nam, which aim to open spaces for community gathering on steps, platforms and boardwalks at different points along the waterfront. Moreover, the integration of WSUD tools such as wetlands for the Sen Pond will create a low-cost water circulation system that could help improve water quality. As WSUD is relatively new for most developing cities in Mekong countries, strong commitment and political leadership, as well as community engagement, may be needed to embrace the concept (ADB, 2019[9]). Countries may also learn from other initiatives around the world that have successfully delivered the benefits of WSUD, such as the Bishan – Ang Mo Kio Park in Singapore (Box 4.1).

Box 4.1. The Kallang river restoration at Bishan – Ang Mo Kio Park, Singapore

Located in the heartlands of Singapore, the Bishan – Ang Mo Kio Park has undergone major upgrades since it was first built in 1988. The latest redevelopment enhances the capacity of the Kallang River that runs through the park. Instead of accommodating a higher flow of storm water in the river through conventional approaches, the Singaporean authority opted for nature-based solutions. This approach increases the capacity of waterway, and also brings more value to wildlife and public users. The project is part of the *Active, Beautiful, Clean Waters* (ABC Waters) Programme, a long-term national initiative launched in 2006 by the Public Utilities Board (PUB) – Singapore's National Water Agency. The programme aims to transform Singapore's canals, rivers and reservoirs. They would move beyond their functions of drainage and water supply into new vibrant spaces that allow people to become stewards of waterways and waterbodies (CLC, 2019[10]). The restoration of the Kallang River at the Bishan – Ang Mo Kio Park was a joint project between PUB and Singapore's National Parks Board.

By integrating the park and the river, the redevelopment project of Bishan – Ang Mo Kio Park has transformed a 2.7-kilometre concrete canal into a 3-kilometre naturalised river. The project employs bioengineering methods such as using different varieties of plants and natural materials along riverbanks. Within the park, riverbanks are gently sloped to allow visitors to walk along the water's edge. The design also allows the riverbanks to serve as a floodplain during heavy rainstorms by channelling storm water to the Marina Reservoir. The park also provides recreational facilities such as playgrounds and the Riverside Gallery, which can be used for community gathering or festive celebrations. In addition, the park, which was completed in 2012, plays an important role in promoting biodiversity. It has become home to diverse flora and fauna. According to (PUB, 2018[11]), several key features of the park include:

- Soil bioengineering techniques: These rely on natural materials, such as plants, stones, branches and roots, to stabilise a river embankment in an ecological and aesthetic manner. Along the canal, soil bioengineering is widely applied to stabilise the slopes of the riverbank and protect them from erosion during storm events. Thanks to this technique, the concrete canal has been transformed into a natural river with landscaped banks that create a riverine habitat and improve urban biodiversity.
- Cleansing biotope: The cleansing biotopes are a form of artificially constructed wetlands. They consist of wetland plants that allow water treatment and purification. Within the park, this feature replaced an existing pond. It allows to filter water that is pumped from the river and the downstream ponds. The filtered water is returned to the ponds and cascades back to the river. Additional UV treatment for the treated water allows water to be made sanitary and used to supply the water playgrounds.
- Vegetated swales: The vegetated swales are natural drainage canals with a mild slope that conveys storm water. Employing vegetated swales can reduce water flow velocities and remove solids such as stones. This particle removal can protect downstream waterways from erosive flows during storms. In the park, the vegetated swales facilitate infiltration, detention and cleaning of storm water runoff before it enters the river.

Source: (PUB, 2018[11]), *ABC Waters Design Guidelines 4th Edition*, Public Utilities Board, Singapore, https://www.pub.gov.sg/Documents/ABC_Waters_Design_Guidelines.pdf.

Community-based solutions for better disaster resilience

Resilience against natural hazards may also depend on the institutional capacity to prepare for disaster effectively. Fragmented sectoral approaches and institutional arrangements could lead to difficulty in implementing disaster risk management at the local level. For instance, co-ordination bodies in Viet Nam have overlapping mandates related to disaster risk management, climate change and water resources management, and can lack authority to act. As a result, many actions developed under inter-ministerial committees are not implemented (World Bank, 2017[12]).

Lack of information and technical skills to put plans into practice also hinder disaster preparedness. Engaging community members may help meet the challenge since they may possess more information about their localities. Through a community-based project, civil society and community-based groups are involved in preparing for disasters, such as collecting and verifying data on local conditions and identifying challenges. In some Mekong countries, they are also involved in decision making. By making use of local knowledge, community-led co-ordinating mechanisms are often cost-effective since they allow local needs and circumstances to be addressed properly (OECD, 2019[1]). This section will discuss country-specific challenges related to community-based disaster risk management, covering examples of community engagement projects for disaster risk resilience in the five Mekong countries.

Cambodia: Strengthening co-ordination across levels of government

The National Committee for Disaster Management (NCDM) is the main government structure for co-ordinating disaster risk reduction (DRR). It consists of various government bodies and representatives of the Royal Cambodian Armed Forces, the Civil Aviation Authority and the key actor of community-based actions – the Cambodian Red Cross (CFE-DMHA, 2017[13]). The country has implemented several community-based programmes; however, limited resources and information sharing with all levels of government may hinder their effectiveness on broader scales.

The Takeo project for flood risk reduction is an example of a community-based solution. The Takeo province of Cambodia is located in a shallow low-lying area in the Mekong Delta. This makes it prone to flooding from Bassac River, Mekong River and canals that link the two. Due to tidal effects, high water levels from both rivers cannot drain easily to the sea. This has caused substantial damage to houses and infrastructure. Flood characteristics have also become more irregular since the completion of a Vietnamese dam downstream. The water could rise faster, stay longer and recede more slowly following water movement at the dam. Besides damage to houses and infrastructure, water levels that remain high could also affect rice production, leaving paddies submerged and unavailable for planting (Pinkaew and Glass, 2007[14]).

To tackle the issue, local and international non-governmental organisations (NGOs) carried out a project to reduce flood risk with the NCDM and the Provincial Committee for Disaster Management. Their roles are mainly to provide the community with information, training, financial and technical assistance. A Village Committee for Disaster Management, which consists of five women and men elected by their communities, implements the project. One activity helps the most vulnerable families to build elevated houses since small bamboo homes are prone to damage by heavy rains, flooding and strong winds. The project involves 13 of the most remote and vulnerable villages and covers 416 families chosen by villagers based on their economic situation and needs. In addition to being involved in decision making, the villagers were also instructed how to raise their homesteads by two to three metres using dirt to elevate the ground above flood level (Pinkaew and Glass, 2007[14]).

This example demonstrates that community-based projects may offer an effective way for training and capacity building at the community level. By strengthening co-ordination between national, provincial and district agencies, the limited implementation of community-based programmes in Cambodia can be expanded to other vulnerable communities.

Lao PDR: Improving central-level involvement in community-based programmes

Community-based DRR programmes in Lao PDR are implemented through the Village Disaster Prevention Units (VDPU) and the Village Disaster Prevention and Control Committees (VDPCC). These institutions aim to increase awareness among local communities. They offer education for community members to learn actions to be taken before, during and after disasters. However, these practices are limited since many villages still do not have VDPU or VDPCC in place (CFE-DMHA, 2017[15]).

The School Flood Safety Programme is another example of a local-level DRR in Lao PDR. It aims to enhance the capacity of communities to cope with floods by empowering young people to take a leadership role as informal communicators. At selected schools, teachers are trained about risk management through workshops organised by the district education offices, and then pass this knowledge on to their students. The programme develops and distributes materials such as booklets and posters. In addition, schools are used as a focal point for activities related to communal training, which also involves parents, women's groups and older community members.

Throughout the implementation process, the Secretariat of the Provincial Disaster Management Committees helps disseminate educational posters, booklets and flood information kits to District Disaster Management Committee members (ADPC, 2015[16]). In other districts, similar programmes use participatory approaches to promote awareness of DRR. Within this programme, teachers underwent an orientation that allowed them to give feedback on pilot modules and learning materials. In this way, teachers' input allowed modules to be revised before potential use in other schools and target locations.

The capacity to manage the risk of disasters varies at the local level due to uneven implementation of the DRR strategy. Some communities are more developed, while others might lag behind. Improving co-ordination and resource allocation from the central level may help meet the challenge.

Myanmar: Developing institutional arrangement at local level

The Myanmar 2017 Action Plan on Disaster Risk Reduction acknowledges community-based disaster resilience as one of its priority actions (MoSWRR, 2017[17]). The plan highlights the role of civil society organisations, foundations and volunteers as key stakeholders to reach the community. Since the concept of DRR is relatively new in Myanmar, community-based programmes are still limited. Moreover, inadequate financial resources along with a lack of institutional arrangements at district or village level have contributed to uneven distribution of these programmes. The relief and resettlement department is limited to the state or division level, making it difficult to reach the village level (CFE-DMHA, 2020[18]). This suggests that developing community-level institutions might help the country strengthen the implementation of its DRR plan.

Drought-resilient farming in the dry zone of Myanmar is an example of the country's few community-based programmes. The dry zone in central Myanmar is a lowland located between the Shan Highlands, the Rakhine Yoma and the Chin Hills. The Ayeyarwady River crosses the region, making it possible to irrigate cultivation alongside the river. A large proportion of the population engages in subsistence rain-fed agriculture or livestock rearing. However, the area has annual rainfall of less than 1 000 millimetres and high evaporation during the dry season due to high temperatures (UNDP, 2019[19]). To strengthen the resilience of subsistence agriculture in this area, Myanmar introduced a participatory rice varietal selection project in 2014. The United Nations Development Programme implemented the project with the Ministry of Natural Resources and Environmental Conservation.

Throughout the project, farmers helped identify high yielding and acceptable rice cultivars for heat tolerance, drought, short duration and salt tolerance. Indeed, farmers' participation may allow better crop selection. They possess experiential knowledge related to the variety of crops such as expected yield, labour availability, seed prices and availability, climatic and soil conditions, and available surface flow (UNDP, 2014[20]). Access to a wider variety of drought-resilient crops is made possible thanks to the establishment of community-level seed banks. The project also assists volunteer farmers in establishing a demonstration plot. This enables them to observe the practicalities and performance of certain varieties before purchasing their preferred seeds from seed banks.

Thailand: Strengthening technical and information capacity

According to the 2015 National Disaster Risk Management Plan of Thailand, community-based disaster risk management is a strategic focus to improve preparedness capacity against natural hazard events (DDPM, 2015[21]). The Department of Disaster Prevention and Mitigation develops and carries out community-based programmes. This national-level government agency delivers education and shares knowledge related to disaster management through the national training institution for disaster management and the community-based volunteer training programme, among others. The agency has also developed the Civil Defence Volunteer network programme, consisting of more than 1 million trained community-based volunteers who are on stand-by to assist government officials during disaster events (Thiprut, 2016[22]).

DRR strategy has been implemented relatively well at the national, provincial and community levels. However, the lack of risk information and data sharing has created challenges for the government to act on DRR measures (Paojinda, 2017[23]). Strengthening the capacity of government officials, community members and other stakeholders to use technology may offer a solution for better data collection and information sharing.

Several community-based measures, whose mechanisms rely on information and data sharing through technology, have been developed at different locations. One example is the innovative water solutions of the Limthong community. Extreme drought during the dry season and severe floods during the rainy season affected Limthong villages repeatedly for 40 years until 2007, damaging houses, roads and agricultural production (Utokapat, 2016[24]). Indeed, the main source of food and income for the community comes from rain-fed agriculture. Since the disasters continually lowered productivity in agriculture, villagers experienced more household debt and migration.

To cope with such an unfavourable situation, the Hydro and Agro Informatics Institute, under the Ministry of Science and Technology Thailand, in partnership with a local NGO, introduced Community Water Resource Management (CWRM). The project allows knowledge and technology transfers between villagers and other stakeholders, enabling them to better analyse, develop and implement CWRM solutions. Throughout implementation, local villagers are first trained to learn and understand new technologies to carry out surveys, collect data and undertake important analysis related to water resources and water balance. The new technologies employed include Global Positioning System, receiver, a telemetering station and satellite images. Moreover, the project promotes traditional knowledge. For instance, elderly people provide information concerning past rainfall and water use, thus helping the community to better understand their water shortage.

According to detailed information collected by villagers, innovative water solutions are developed jointly with expert stakeholders. Considering the geo-social condition of the village, the solutions consisted of pond network system and canal streets. The pond network system aims to reduce flood and increase water storage during the two different seasons. Meanwhile, the canal streets are used as a waterway and distribution system that delivers floodwater to the ponds. The network is maintained by a CWRM Committee, which has local members and operates under the local government.

The 42.2 kilometres of canals that connect with a network of more than 100 ponds can increase water storage by 1.16 million cubic metres (MCM), enough to supply 68% of agricultural land in the area (Utokapat, 2016[24]). In addition, the system allows full protection from flood and drought for an area of 11.76 km^2 and reduces the risk of both disasters in another 21.34 km^2. With such benefits, other communities expanded the network significantly in less than ten years. More than 2 200 households in an area of 278.25 km^2 currently benefit from the system, compared to the 15 households in an area of 5.9 km^2 that participated at its initial stage (Utokapat, 2016[24]).

Viet Nam: Promoting effectiveness and sustainability of community-based programmes

In Viet Nam, the government has tried to improve community-based disaster risk management (CBDRM) through laws and national strategies. For instance, the law on natural disaster prevention and control took effect in May 2014. It outlines regulations for natural disaster prevention at national, local and community levels, and defines roles and responsibilities of relevant bodies (CFE-DMHA, 2018[25]). Programmes related to CBDRM fall under the Ministry of Agriculture and Rural Development.

Some projects that adopt top-down approaches might not be able to bolster local resilience effectively. Indeed, several past experiences demonstrated that bottom-up approaches of CBDRM have been effective at increasing community awareness. Community-based mangrove management in Da Loc and Nga Thuy communes in Thanh Hoa province are two examples of the positive outcomes of CBDRM. For local residents, the degradation could increase the risk of exposure to more serious storms and tidal floods. For instance, after Typhoon Damrey (in 2005) brought tidal waves and upstream floods, damaging 100 houses, destroying shrimp farms and 500 hectares of crops and contaminating soils with salt water (CARE, 2016[26]), many projects took place in the area, aiming to restore the mangrove forest. However, local participation was limited. In particular, private contractors or local authorities often managed the planting, maintenance and protection phases (CARE, 2016[26]). This resulted in reduced awareness among local communities, and a low survival rate of mangroves due to inappropriate planting.

In 2007, a community-based approach for strengthening coastal resilience was introduced. Non-governmental organisations (NGOs), private actors and the government joined forces in a partnership to implement the project. The Community-Based Mangrove Management Boards (CMMB) was formed, composed of representatives elected from the Commune People's Committee and mass organisations. Its main role consists of steering planning and decision making for the planting, maintenance and protection of young mangrove forests. Moreover, the project provides training for village-level facilitators, which could enable them to support assessments of vulnerabilities and to develop disaster preparedness plans.

With strong support from the local government, CMMB has mobilised community members to contribute their time, knowledge and labour to mangrove restoration and disaster preparedness planning. Since 2007, trained local facilitators have developed disaster preparedness plans in 28 villages. They are revised annually with help from community members (CARE, 2016[26]). In addition, 458 hectares of mangrove forests have been planted. These forests have a survival rate of 70-90%, a significantly higher rate compared to previous projects in the same area where survival rates ranged from 10% to 50%. Participation of community members throughout all phases of restoration activities has also strengthened their sense of responsibility. For instance, in 2011, community members immediately reported the mangrove encroachment by clam farmers to local authorities (CARE, 2016[26]). This example highlights that community participation may help ensure the sustainability of community-based projects.

The use of digital tools as an effective early warning system

Advancements in technology, such as artificial intelligence, the Internet of Things, Big Data and drones create new possibilities to develop low-cost digital tools for early warning systems. These tools could offer better quality and timeliness in transferring information, analysing, monitoring, assessing risk and forecasting. This, in turn, would allow for better awareness and preparedness against disasters. However, large technological gaps remain between early warning systems used in developing and developed countries (OECD, 2019[11]).

Among digital tools for early warning systems, mobile phone use has gained importance in developing countries. In the Mekong region, mobile-cellular telephone subscriptions have increased significantly. As of 2018, the number of mobile-telephone subscriptions exceeded the number of inhabitants for all Mekong countries except for Lao PDR (Figure 4.4). This presents an opportunity to use mobile phones as key components of early warning systems.

Figure 4.4. Mobile-cellular telephone subscriptions per 100 inhabitants in Mekong countries

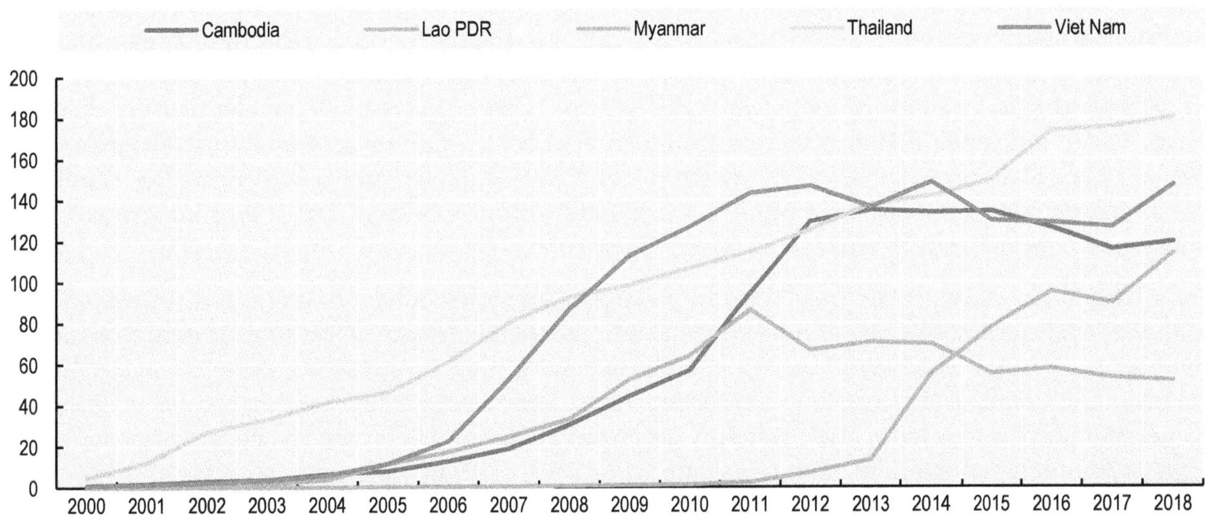

StatLink https://doi.org/10.1787/888934167695

Source: (ITU, 2020[27]), *ICT Statistics* (database), www.itu.int/en/ITU-D/Statistics/Pages/stat/default.aspx.

Each country in the Mekong region has developed its own early warning phone service. For instance, the EWS1294 introduced in 2013 allows Cambodians to receive early warning messages from the NCDM. Users can simply dial 1294 to register, which indicates their location. In an emergency, such as floods or storms, users in the affected area receive an audio message. It warns them about potential risks and advises them on the steps to take to protect themselves. These steps can include evacuation to the nearest safe site, staying indoors or securing their livestock (UNDP, 2019[28]).

While Lao PDR's SMS warning system is still in its initial stages, a pilot project was launched in early 2019. Four Laotian private telecommunications companies contributed to the project by sending SMS (text) messages related to weather conditions. This information is provided by the Department of Meteorology and Hydrology of the Ministry of Natural Resources and Environment (UNDP, 2019[29]). In Myanmar, the government-owned mobile phone application, Disaster Alert Notification (DAN), sends disaster-related information to smartphone users. The application's features include news and early warning notifications, updates on DRR activities, emergency contact numbers, advice, and direct links to a government website for real-time weather forecasts (MoSWRR, 2016[30]).

In Thailand, the *Warning Volunteer Networking*, or *Mr. Warning*, contributes to rapid dissemination of warning messages among villagers through mobile phones. Mr. Warning is a warning team at local or community level trained to monitor the situation, warn the public, and co-ordinate evacuation. Locals and officials set up a group chat to communicate with each other. By exchanging information with local networks, officials can better estimate the risks and identify potential damages (ADPC, 2015[31]). As of 2017, there are nearly 28 000 members of Mr. Warning in 3 340 risk-prone villages (DDPM, 2017[32]).

Similar early warning systems can be found in the coastal provinces of Thua Thien Hue, Quang Nam and Da Nang, Viet Nam. In the past, village leaders would disseminate disaster-related information through loudspeakers in public spaces or door-to-door (SCI, 2016[33]). However, such methods are inadequate due to power cuts or limited coverage of the loudspeaker systems. In 2016, the free SMS early warning system was introduced. This allowed volunteers, who are household heads and members of community disaster action teams, to share information with the government regarding floodwater levels they monitor in their neighbourhoods. This mechanism enables government to improve data collection, mapping and decision making. In case of emergency, anyone registered with the system receives SMS warnings and advice to protect themselves.

Despite improved early warning systems, messages often do not reach across the country, especially to remote vulnerable areas that are often most at risk. Rapid development of new dams by upstream countries in the Mekong region often affects water availability and quantity in downstream nations. Indeed, water level at downstream locations is controlled by the storage, withdrawal and release decisions of upstream nations. When a disaster affecting a dam occurs in one country, the impact can be transboundary. For instance, the 2018 dam collapse in southern Lao PDR brought extensive flooding to Cambodia. Widespread damage was inevitable since Cambodia did not have access to real-time information about the increased risk of flooding (Hossain et al., 2019[34]).

Efforts have been made to address concerns regarding the transboundary nature of disasters affecting dams. Viet Nam recently launched a satellite-based operational system. With support from international partners, the system was developed to improve timely access to upstream reservoir information in transboundary river basins of the Red and Mekong rivers. The satellite data allow users to calculate storage volume change of a reservoir. They can also get information on how a dam operates within any month thanks to the record of average storage volume (UNOOSA, 2019[35]). More can be done to make use of these satellite data and transform them into accessible tools for an improved transboundary early warning system.

Addressing water challenges amid the COVID-19 pandemic

More recently, COVID-19 has been rapidly spreading across the globe, creating a much bigger external shock than natural disasters that disrupt various sectors (OECD, 2020[36]). The outbreak highlights the importance of safe and reliable water supply since frequent handwashing is one of the most recommended measures to minimise the spread of the virus. However, as of 2017, nearly 40% of the world's population lack access to basic handwashing. Among the five Mekong countries, Lao PDR lags behind with around 50% of its population lacking adequate access to handwashing with soap and water (Figure 4.5).

Figure 4.5. Population using a handwashing facility with soap and water (percentage) in Mekong countries, 2017

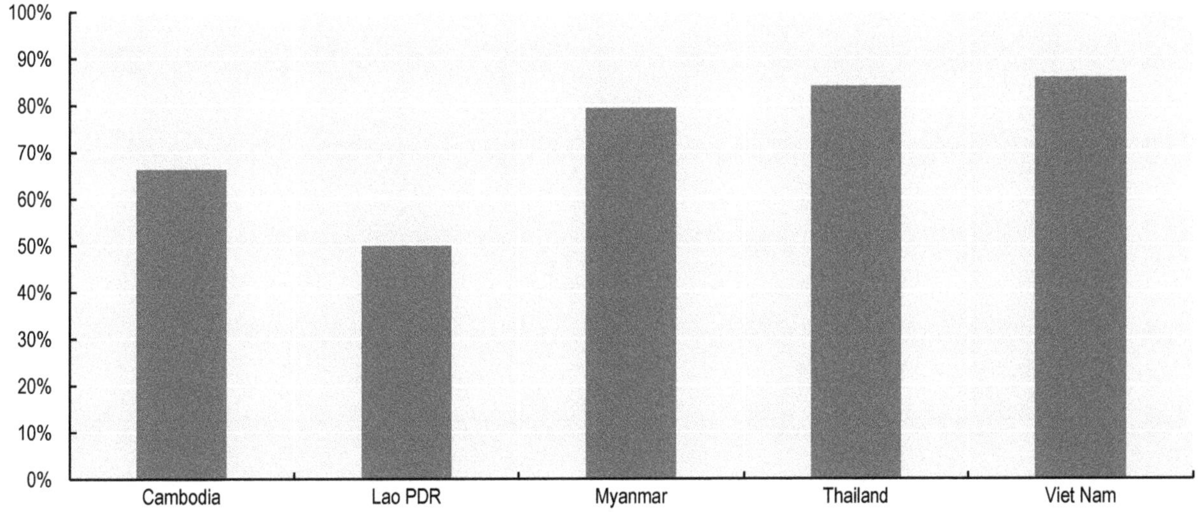

StatLink https://doi.org/10.1787/888934167714

Source: (WHO-UNICEF, 2020[37]), Joint Monitoring Programme for Water Supply, Sanitation and Hygiene (database), https://sdg6data.org/tables.

In addition to the lack of basic handwashing facilities, the Mekong countries need to improve access to safe drinking water. This is especially the case for Cambodia, Lao PDR and Myanmar, where some population groups still rely on unimproved sources of drinking water or collect surface water (Figure 4.6). Summer droughts may exacerbate the lack of access to safe and reliable water during the COVID-19 pandemic, posing serious threats to domestic water use. For instance, in Viet Nam, the 2019-20 drought and saltwater intrusion greatly affected people living in the coastal districts of Tran De, Long Phu and Vinh Chau. In particular, these events affected those not connected to the centralised water supply works. Saltwater intrusion has affected surface water and the depleted groundwater is unable to meet water needs, resulting in more than 26 500 households lacking water for domestic use (MARD, 2020[38]). In Sittwe township of Rakhine State, Myanmar, summer drought has led to acute water shortages, leaving individuals with a lack of access to adequate water. This, in turn, makes it difficult for them to practise the most basic measures to prevent the spread of COVID-19 (Shwe, Pru and Prasad, 2020[39]).

Figure 4.6. Household drinking water coverage in Mekong countries, by service levels, 2017

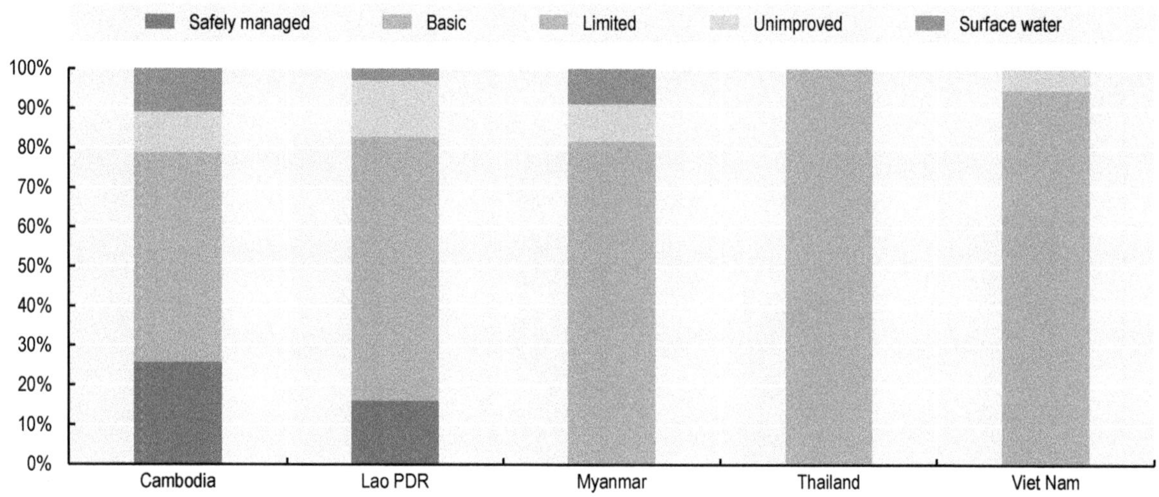

StatLink https://doi.org/10.1787/888934167733

Note: "Safely managed" indicates that drinking water collection is from an improved water source located on the premises, available when needed and free from faecal and priority chemical contamination. "Basic" indicates that drinking water collection is from an improved source, provided collection time is not more than 30 minutes for a roundtrip including queuing. "Limited" indicates that drinking water is from an improved source for which collection time exceeds 30 minutes for a roundtrip, including queuing. "Unimproved sources" are unprotected wells or springs. "Surface water" indicates that drinking water is collected directly from a river, dam, lake, pond, stream, canal or irrigation canal.
Source: (WHO-UNICEF, 2020[40]), *Joint Monitoring Programme for Water Supply, Sanitation and Hygiene* (database), https://washdata.org/data/household.

Where communities live far away from piped water, people tend to purchase fresh water. During episodes of summer drought, however, price increases reflect increased scarcity. Due to water scarcity, as well as a lack of appropriate facilities, people tend to reduce the frequency of basic hygiene and sanitation practices or abandon them altogether. This increases the risk of exposure to pathogens. In Viet Nam, local authorities have responded to these hazards by purchasing and transporting water to people affected by drought, drilling more wells, and building more public faucets and tanks to provide water for domestic use (MARD, 2020[41]).

Within urban settings, people living in densely populated areas, especially informal settlements, can also be at greater risk during the coronavirus outbreak. Physical distancing is nearly impossible. Moreover, these settlements are often not connected to basic municipal services, particularly piped water, sanitation facilities, and drainage and treatment networks. For instance, in Yangon, Myanmar, slums often depend on ponds or public tube wells for water supply. Water extracted from these sources is prone to high levels of pollution due to the flow of waste (UN HABITAT, 2020[42]). People also rely on private and informal water providers, whose services are often expensive and unreliable. During the pandemic, many slum residents lost their jobs. Their limited household budgets make it difficult to afford safe water. Moreover, sanitation facilities are mostly limited to open pit latrines. By relying on communal water points and sanitation facilities, people queuing for access in close proximity to others makes physical distancing hard to implement.

Besides water and sanitation challenges, informal settlements are susceptible to risk of flooding on a near daily basis since they are located along rivers, on swamp land or on the riverbed (UN HABITAT, 2020[42]). Disaster preparedness and response plans are often absent, making slums more vulnerable when disaster strikes. Living conditions, along with daily flooding and other natural hazards, could increase the prevalence of vector- and water-borne diseases such as diarrhoea, dysentery, malaria and tuberculosis. This, in turn, may lead to low immunity and increase the risk of exposure to COVID-19. Indeed, the share of urban slum population is positively correlated with the mortality rate caused by unsafe water, sanitation and hygiene (WASH) services (Figure 4.7). This should alarm policy makers and prompt them to address unequal access to water, particularly in densely populated urban areas and to consider integrating the previously discussed WSUD for better disaster resilience.

Figure 4.7. Urban slum population and mortality rate attributable to unsafe WASH service in Mekong countries, 2016

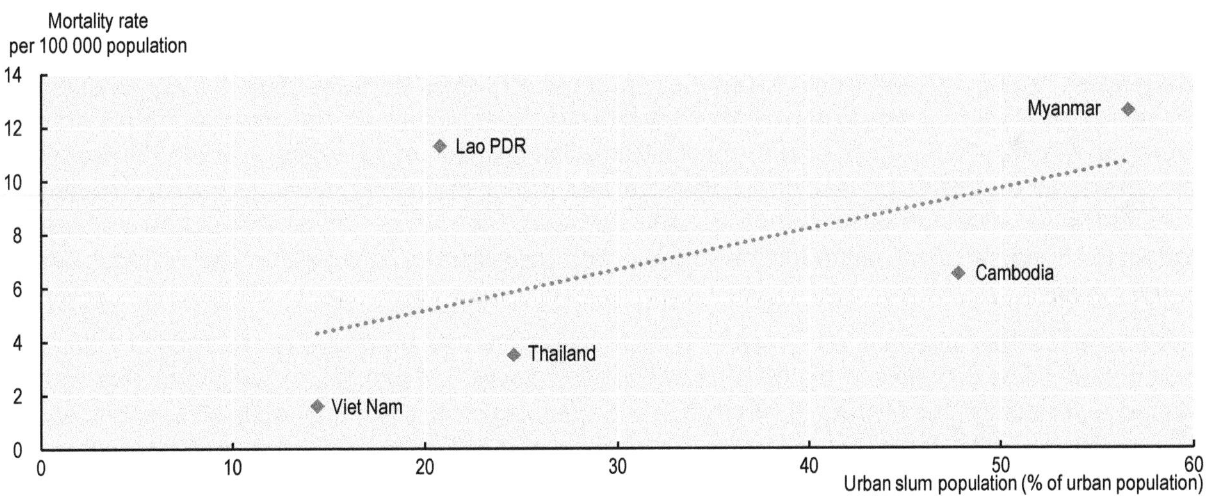

StatLink https://doi.org/10.1787/888934167752

Source: (UNESCAP, 2020[43]), *SDG Indicators Data* (database), https://dataexplorer.unescap.org.

Boosting disaster resilience in the midst of the COVID-19 crisis

The COVID-19 outbreak has affected large-scale infrastructure projects, especially hydropower dam projects along the Mekong River and its tributaries. These projects are at risk of delays and shutdowns due to lockdown, movement restrictions and fear of contagion. For instance, in Lao PDR, the government temporarily halted all hydropower construction following the positive test of a mining company worker for COVID-19 (Board, 2020[44]). Consultations on the major Luang Prabang dam have also been postponed. In Viet Nam, energy projects are at risk of delay due to travel bans that prevent executives, engineers and planners from foreign oil and gas companies from visiting. These delays may cause further blackouts across the country since Viet Nam is already facing growing electricity outages due to lack of new power generation plants (Daiss, 2020[45]). Given the interrelationship between water and electricity, it could be challenging for Viet Nam to supply water if the crisis persists. Indeed, electricity is needed for the pumping, treatment and distribution of water, as well as for the collection, treatment and discharge of wastewater (Copeland and Carter, 2017[46]). As of 22 May 2020, the Vietnamese government was reportedly strengthening campaigns to raise awareness on water and energy conservation in response to droughts and water shortages that might occur more often (VNS, 2020[47]).

As large-scale infrastructure projects are at risk of delays, small-scale projects with dual objectives are emerging. Such projects aim to increase resilience when disaster occurs, while dealing with the socio-economic impact of COVID-19. For instance, in Thailand, people who lost their jobs during the pandemic have been hired to develop irrigation systems and other water infrastructure. In so doing, they are helping farmers deal with the water crisis, while maintaining incomes. Around 500 workers, who are paid about the same as their normal wage, will develop 103 water projects in three drought-stricken provinces (Theparat and Charoensuthipan, 2020[48]).

Apart from dealing with infrastructure, governments need to ensure hygiene guidelines reach all layers of communities, especially those not connected to pipe systems, who therefore need to buy water. In rural Cambodia, for instance, many households are burdened with self-collection and self-treatment of their own drinking water, relying on water kiosks to buy drinking water. However, because of the COVID-19 outbreak, water kiosk clients are reluctant to leave their homes to buy water, and kiosk staff are insecure about safety in their jobs (Highton, 2020[49]). To ensure continuity in water distribution, Cambodia is raising communities' awareness about COVID-19 prevention. These initiatives include promoting measures such as maintaining physical distance, wearing masks and using hand sanitiser. The role of community leaders may also be important to strengthen compliance with basic prevention measures for activities that require close contact between people.

Mobile phones can also play an important part in raising community awareness about COVID-19. During this difficult period, some countries in the Mekong region have developed mobile applications to help fight the pandemic. For instance, the Ministry of Information and Communications and the Health Ministry of Viet Nam developed *Ncovi*. This application serves as a channel for delivering all formal medical notices and announcements to citizens, allowing them to adjust their activities accordingly. Another Vietnamese innovation is the *Bluezone* application that uses Bluetooth Low Energy technology to pinpoint the location of a mobile phone within two metres. If the phone's owner tests positive for COVID-19, the Bluezone will use the contact history of the infected person to deliver warnings to other users who have high risk of coming into contact with them (MIC, 2020[50]). Thailand has developed the *Mor Chana* mobile app, which uses GPS and Bluetooth technology to track locations of people who test positive for COVID-19. It can also help health authorities identify those who have been in close contact with infected people (Silva, 2020[51]).

Conclusion

The vulnerability of the Mekong region to natural hazards has required strengthening disaster preparedness to minimise damage and avoid reversing the development gains. Efforts can take two complementary approaches. Promoting multi-purpose and nature-based solutions can improve hard infrastructure, while institutional collaboration and community engagement can strengthen soft infrastructure. Joint planning between countries and cross-country initiatives are needed since the impact of water-related hazards is often transboundary. There is scope for improving the use of technology for better disaster risk resilience, especially to prevent transboundary disasters.

The COVID-19 outbreak has brought to light the need for integrated disaster risk reduction plans for pandemics, as well as for natural hazards. During pandemics, more handwashing might increase demand for water. As countries may face future natural disasters and pandemics, the important role played by proper hygiene in slowing the spread of COVID-19 provides a critical lesson. Countries need to accelerate the development of resilient and sustainable water infrastructure and improve its availability. Indeed, this should be a priority in order to ensure that reliable and safe water remains accessible and widespread even during challenging times.

References

ADB (2019), *Nature Based Solutions for Cities in Viet Nam: Water Sensitive Urban Design*, Asian Development Bank, Manila, http://www.adb.org/sites/default/files/publication/535016/nature-based-solutions-cities-viet-nam.pdf. [9]

ADPC (2015), *Bringing Collaborative Governance in Community Early Warning System for Flood Risk Reduction*, Asian Disaster Preparedness Center, Bangkok, http://www.adpc.net/igo/category/ID1060/doc/2016-w0Re72-ADPC-Bringing_Collaborative_for_print.pdf. [31]

ADPC (2015), *Empowering Communities and Strengthening Resilience: Lao PDR*, Asian Disaster Preparedness Center, Bangkok, http://www.adpc.net/igo/category/ID1001/doc/2015-cHWj0N-ADPC-Lao_doc_for_upload.pdf. [16]

ASEAN (2017), *Executive Summary Report: ROK-ASEAN Cooperation Project on Building Resilience for Sustainable ASEAN from Water-related Disasters*, Association of Southeast Asian Nations, Jakarta, http://environment.asean.org/wp-content/uploads/2018/04/Building-Resilience-for-Sustainable-ASEAN-from-Water-Related-Disasters_Executive-Summary-Report_small.pdf. [2]

Board, J. (2020), "Southeast Asia's hydropower boom grinds to a halt as Covid-19 stalls projects", *Channel News Asia*, Singapore, http://www.channelnewsasia.com/news/asia/southeast-asia-hydropower-boom-covid-19-coronavirus-12652202 (accessed on 13 May 2020). [44]

CARE (2016), *Building Coastal Resilience in Viet Nam: An Integrated, Community-based Approach to Mangrove Management, Disaster Risk Reduction and Climate Change Adaptation*, CARE, https://careclimatechange.org/wp-content/uploads/2016/02/Building-Coastal-Resilience-in-Vietnam.pdf. [26]

CFE-DMHA (2020), *Myanmar: Disaster Management Reference Handbook*, Center for Excellence in Disaster Management and Human Assistance, Honolulu, https://reliefweb.int/sites/reliefweb.int/files/resources/disaster-mgmt-ref-hdbk-burma_0.pdf. [18]

CFE-DMHA (2018), *Vietnam: Disaster Management Reference Handbook*, Center for Excellence in Disaster Management and Human Assistance, Honolulu, https://reliefweb.int/sites/reliefweb.int/files/resources/2018%20Vietnam%20Disaster%20Management%20Reference%20Handbook.pdf. [25]

CFE-DMHA (2017), *Lao PDR: Disaster Management Reference Handbook*, Center for Excellence in Disaster Management and Human Assistance, Honolulu, https://reliefweb.int/sites/reliefweb.int/files/resources/CFE%20DM%20Reference%20Handbook-Lao%20PDR%202017.pdf. [15]

CFE-DMHA (2017), *Cambodia: Disaster Management Reference Handbook*, Center for Excellence in Disaster Management and Human Assistance, Honolulu, https://reliefweb.int/sites/reliefweb.int/files/resources/CFE%20DM%20Reference%20Handbook-Cambodia%202017.pdf. [13]

CLC (2019), *"Active, Beautiful, Clean Waters (ABC Waters) Programme"*, Infopedia, Centre for Liveable Cities, Singapore, https://eresources.nlb.gov.sg/infopedia/articles/SIP_2019-08-21_203240.html (accessed on 13 May 2020). [10]

Copeland, C. and N. Carter (2017), *Energy-Water Nexus: The Water Sector's Energy Use*, Congressional Research Service Report R432000, Washington, DC, https://fas.org/sgp/crs/misc/R43200.pdf. [46]

CRED (2020), *Emergency Events Database (database)*, http://www.emdat.be/ (accessed on 9 May 2020). [4]

Daiss, T. (2020), "Covid-19 knocking the lights out in Viet Nam", *Asia Times*, https://asiatimes.com/2020/03/covid-19-knocking-the-lights-out-in-vietnam/. [45]

DDPM (2017), "DDPM enhances networking capacity building in disaster prevention and mitigation for promoting Safety Thailand", Department of Disaster Prevention and Mitigation, Bangkok, http://www.disaster.go.th/en/cdetail-8322-disaster_news-199-1/. [32]

DDPM (2015), *National Disaster Risk Management Plan 2015*, Department of Disaster Prevention and Mitigation, Bangkok, http://www.disaster.go.th/upload/download/file_attach/584115d64fcee.pdf. [21]

Highton, R. (2020), "Integrating fish conservation with water sanitation during COVID-19 in Cambodia", The Fish Tank blog, http://blog.worldfishcenter.org/2020/05/integrating-fish-conservation-with-water-sanitation-during-covid-19-in-cambodia/. [49]

Hossain, F. et al. (2019), "When Floods Cross Borders, Satellite Data Can Help", *Eos*, Vol. 100, http://dx.doi.org/10.1029/2019eo115775. [34]

ICOLD (2014), *International Commission on Large Dams (website)*, http://www.icold-cigb.org (accessed on 13 May 2020). [5]

ITU (2020), *ICT Statistics (database)*, http://www.itu.int/en/ITU-D/Statistics/Pages/stat/default.aspx (accessed on 18 May 2020). [27]

MARD (2020), "Nearly 26,000 households in Khanh Hoa are at risk of domestic water shortage", Ministry of Agriculture and Rural Development, Ha Noi, http://phongchongthientai.mard.gov.vn/en/Pages/nearly-26-000-households-in-khanh-hoa-are-at-risk-of-domestic-water-shortage.aspx?item=undefined. [41]

MARD (2020), "Reduce damage by actively responding to drought during the 2019-2020 dry season", Ministry of Agriculture and Rural Development, Ha Noi, http://phongchongthientai.mard.gov.vn/en/Pages/reduce-damage-by-actively-responding-to-drought-during-the-2019-2020-dry-season.aspx. [38]

MIC (2020), "Technology tremendously boosts Covid-19 fight in Vietnam", Ministry of Information and Communications, Ha Noi, https://english.mic.gov.vn/Pages/TinTuc/141918/Technology-tremendously-boosts-Covid-19-fight-in-Vietnam.html. [50]

MoSWRR (2017), "Myanmar Action Plan on Disaster Risk Reduction", Ministry of Social Welfare, Relief and Resettlement, Naypyitaw, http://themimu.info/sites/themimu.info/files/documents/Core_Doc_Myanmar_Action_Plan_on_Disaster_Risk_Reduction_2017.PDF. [17]

MoSWRR (2016), "Tool for the effectiveness of early warning information: Disaster Alert Notification (DAN), mobile app for disaster communication", presentation, Ministry of Social Welfare, Relief and Resettlement, Naypyitaw, https://myanmar.gov.mm/documents/20143/0/DAN+Mobile+App+for+IDDR.pdf/0d3128f5-f780-518f-1c67-2b0e4c157bbc?t=1529724183184. [30]

MRC (2017), "Transboundary Water Resources Management Issues in the Mekong Delta", Mekong River Commission, Vientiane, http://www.mrcmekong.org/assets/Publications/MEKONG-DELTA-Issue-paper-7-Sep-17-for-web.pdf. [8]

OECD (2020), *Economic Outlook for Southeast Asia, China and India 2020 – Update: Meeting the Challenges of COVID-19*, OECD Publishing, Paris, https://dx.doi.org/10.1787/e8c90b68-en. [36]

OECD (2019), *Economic Outlook for Southeast Asia, China and India 2020: Rethinking Education for the Digital Era*, OECD Publishing, Paris, https://dx.doi.org/10.1787/1ba6cde0-en. [1]

OECD (2017), *Multi-Purpose Water Infrastructure: Recommendations to maximise economic benefits*, OECD Policy Perspectives, OECD, Paris, http://www.oecd.org/environment/outreach/MPWI_Perspectives_Final_WEB.pdf. [6]

Paojinda (2017), "Thailand's official statement by H.E. Anupong Paojinda", presentation to the 5th global platform for disaster risk reduction, Cancun, http://www.preventionweb.net/files/globalplatform/5GPDRR%20Official%20statement%20-%20THAILAND%20updated.pdf. [23]

Pinkaew, T. and A. Glass (2007), *Community-based Disaster Risk Reduction Programme in Cambodia*, Oxfam International, http://www.humanitarianlibrary.org/resource/community-based-disaster-risk-reduction-programme-cambodia-0. [14]

PUB (2018), *ABC Waters Design Guidelines 4th Edition*, Public Utilities Board, Singapore, http://www.pub.gov.sg/Documents/ABC_Waters_Design_Guidelines.pdf. [11]

SCI (2016), "How SMS technology can ensure education continuity: Early warning system innovations in Viet Nam", Save the Children International, https://scasia.exposure.co/how-sms-technology-can-ensure-education-continuity. [33]

Shwe, N., T. Pru and V. Prasad (2020), "Preventing Coronavirus: Public hand-washing stations to combat Covid-19 in Sittwe", United Nations Human Settlements Programme, Yangon, https://unhabitat.org.mm/news/public-hand-washing-stations-to-combat-covid-19-in-sittwe/. [39]

Silva, M. (2020), *Covid-19 Apps*, European Emergency Number Association, Brussels, https://eena.org/document/covid-19-apps/. [51]

Theparat, C. and P. Charoensuthipan (2020), "Royal water project to reinvigorate farming", *Bangkok Post*, Bangkok, http://www.bangkokpost.com/thailand/general/1913408/royal-water-project-to-reinvigorate-farming. [48]

Thiprut, S. (2016), *Thailand Country Report 2016*, Asian Disaster Reduction Center – Visiting Researcher Program, Bangkok, http://www.adrc.asia/countryreport/THA/2016/Thailand_CR2016B.pdf. [22]

UN HABITAT (2020), "Housing at the forefront of the response to COVID-19", Discussion Paper on Policy Options for Myanmar, United Nations Human Settlements Programme, Yangon, https://unhabitat.org.mm/wp-content/uploads/2020/05/COVID-19-Discussion-Paper-on-Policy-Options-for-Myanmar_UN-Habitat.pdf. [42]

UNDP (2019), "Dial 1294: UNDP and People in Need expand early warning phone service in Cambodia", United Nations Development Programme, Phnom Penh, http://www.adaptation-undp.org/dial-1294-undp-and-people-need-expand-early-warning-phone-service-cambodia. [28]

UNDP (2019), "Spreading the word of warning in Southern Laos to ensure we leave no one behind", United Nations Development Programme, Vientiane, http://www.la.undp.org/content/lao_pdr/en/home/presscenter/articles/2019/03/spreading-the-word-of-warning-in-southern-laos-to-ensure-we-leav.html. [29]

UNDP (2019), *Terminal Evaluation Report: Addressing Climate Change Risks on Water Resources & Food Security in the Dry Zone of Myanmar*, United Nations Development Programme, https://erc.undp.org/evaluation/documents/detail/13739. [19]

UNDP (2014), "Project document: Addressing climate change risks on water resources & food security in the dry zone of Myanmar", United Nations Development Programme, https://info.undp.org/docs/pdc/Documents/MMR/MMR_AF_Prodoc_10_Mar_2014.pdf. [20]

UNESCAP (2020), *SDG Indicators Data (database)*, https://dataexplorer.unescap.org (accessed on 22 May 2020). [43]

UNESCO, UN-WATER (2020), *United Nations World Water Development Report 2020: Water and Climate Change*, UNESCO, Paris, https://unesdoc.unesco.org/ark:/48223/pf0000372985/PDF/372985eng.pdf.multi. [3]

UNOOSA (2019), "Satellite data powers flood early warning system", United Nations Office for Outer Space Affairs, Vienna, http://www.un-spider.org/news-and-events/news/satellite-data-powers-flood-early-warning-system. [35]

Utokapat (2016), *Application of Science and Technology for Community Water-Related Disaster Risk Reduction*, Utokapat Foundation under Royal Patronage of H.M. the King, Bangkok, http://www.preventionweb.net/files/51880_wrdrrbook1.pdf. [24]

VNS (2020), "PM calls for urgent action on drought, saltwater intrusion", *Viet Nam News*, Ha Noi, https://vietnamnews.vn/environment/717097/pm-calls-for-urgent-action-on-drought-saltwater-intrusion.html (accessed on 13 May 2020). [47]

WHO-UNICEF (2020), *Joint Monitoring Programme for Water Supply, Sanitation and Hygiene (database)*, https://washdata.org/data/household (accessed on 2 May 2020). [40]

WHO-UNICEF (2020), *Joint Monitoring Programme for Water Supply, Sanitation and Hygiene (database)*, https://sdg6data.org/tables (accessed on 2 May 2020). [37]

WLE Greater Mekong (2018), *CGIAR Research Program on Water, Land and Ecosystems – Greater Mekong (website)*, https://wle-mekong.cgiar.org/changes/our-research/greater-mekong-dams-observatory/ (accessed on 13 May 2020). [7]

World Bank (2017), *Toward Integrated Disaster Risk Management in Vietnam*, World Bank, Washington, DC, http://documents.worldbank.org/curated/en/761091508230982951/pdf/120444-REVISED-PUBLIC-17027-Vietnam-Strategy-OVERVIEW-Sep12-2017.pdf. [12]

5 Challenges of water regulation in the Mekong region

Universal access to drinking safe water, sanitation and hygiene can provide benefits to health, well-being, the economy and the environment. However, the Mekong region faces a number of challenges, including financing the water infrastructure needed to meet the demands of growing economies and populations. This chapter explores the characteristics of good water and wastewater regulations before turning to priorities in Mekong countries: Cambodia, Lao People's Democratic Republic, Myanmar, Thailand and Viet Nam. This chapter addresses issues such as financial sustainability, quality standards, law enforcement, public service obligations, delivery standards, risk management, incentives for more efficient water use in agriculture, public-private partnerships, water demand management, information gathering, licensing, public participation, dispute resolution and consumer protection.

Introduction

Economic growth in the Mekong region is expected to stay solid in the medium term, although currently disrupted by the COVID-19 outbreak (OECD, 2020[1]). In line with the growing economies and populations, the region is experiencing an increasing demand for infrastructure. Indeed, from 2016 to 2040 inclusive, an estimated USD 605 billion in infrastructure investment will be needed in Viet Nam, USD 494 billion in Thailand, USD 224 billion in Myanmar and USD 87 billion in Cambodia (Oxford Economics and Global Infrastructure Hub, 2017[2]). Developing infrastructure, as well as expanding and upgrading existing infrastructure, will be critical in further driving growth and development in the Mekong region.

Although water has been an important component of many parts of daily life and the economy in the Mekong region, water infrastructure has not received much attention. Lack of financing and co-ordination among actors are key challenges for water infrastructure. All four Mekong countries reviewed in a 2017 report – Cambodia, Lao People's Democratic Republic (hereafter "Lao PDR"), Thailand and Viet Nam – lacked financing to meet national water targets (UNESCO WWAP (United Nations World Water Assessment Programme), 2017[3]).

Characteristics of good water and wastewater regulations

The water and wastewater services (WWS) sector has several common characteristics. It is a monopolistic sector, in general; it produces different information; and it generates externalities such as pollution. Regulators could play a role in addressing the following areas in order to ensure effective water regulations (OECD, 2015[4]):

- Addressing "market failures" of WWS so the sector can fully meet public interest for all actors involved at the least cost.
- Setting quality standards for drinking water and wastewater treatment to protect public health.
- Promoting easy and transparent access to data. As service providers, water operators usually possess information that is rarely accessible to public authorities and customers.
- Balancing the economic, social and environmental aspects of WWS, ensuring delivery in accordance with the principles of universality, continuity, quality of services, equality of access, affordability and transparency.
- Enhancing co-ordination among actors. At the horizontal level, different ministries regulate various aspects of WWS. As an example, setting and monitoring water quality standards may fall under the purview of the health ministry, water pollution under environment, and regulation of tariffs and investment under economics or finance. At the vertical level, municipalities sometimes manage WWS delivery.

This chapter will discuss 19 points for countries in the Mekong region, covering a wide range of roles performed by WWS regulators, shown in Table 5.1.

Table 5.1. Typology of regulatory functions for WWS

Type of regulatory functions	Definition
Tariff regulation	Establishing a tariff methodology and/or setting and updating prices or supervising the tariff-setting process, determining tariffs by consumer group, establishing caps on revenues or rate of return on investment.
Quality standard for drinking water	Setting quality standards for drinking water and/or monitoring compliance.
Quality standard for wastewater treatment	Setting quality standards for wastewater treatment and wastewater discharges and/or monitoring compliance.
Defining public service obligations/social regulation	Setting public service obligations (including requirements on access to services) and performance requirements for operators.
Defining technical/industry and service standards	Developing the standards that underpin the technical modalities and level of service delivery.
Setting incentives for efficient use of water resources	Establishing incentives or specific schemes to promote efficient water resource use.
Setting incentives for efficient investment	Establishing incentives or specific schemes to promote efficient investment.
Promoting innovative technologies	Establishing incentives or specific schemes to promote innovative technologies.
Promoting demand management	Establishing incentives or specific schemes to promote reduced water demand.
Analysing water utilities' investment plans/business plans	In some cases, the regulator may be asked to approve the business plan or the investment plan of utilities.
Information and data gathering	Collecting data from operators and undertaking market research to identify trends and potential risks.
Monitoring of service delivery performance	Monitoring of the performance of water services against a set of targets or of performance indicators. This can involve the benchmarking of water utilities.
Licensing of water operators	Granting or approving licences for the operation of water systems.
Supervision of contracts with utilities/private actors	The obligations granted by public authorities to a specific utility may be detailed in a specific contract (it is usually the case when a private actor is brought in). The regulator may be tasked with the supervision of the contract.
Supervising utilities' financing activities	Monitoring the financial schemes of water utilities (e.g. bond issuance, equity investments).
Carrying management audits on utilities	Auditing and/or approving the business plans of utilities.
Customer engagement	Consulting with customers on regulatory issues; communicating regulatory decisions to the public.
Consumer protection and dispute resolution	Handling consumer complaints about regulated entities.
Advice and advocacy	Providing advice for policy making and project implementation; identifying opportunities for reforms; encouraging improvements to the regulatory framework.

Source: OECD (2015[4]), *The Governance of Water Regulators*, OECD Studies on Water, OECD Publishing, Paris.

Functions, roles and scope of activities

Water and wastewater regulators are usually part of a broad regulatory framework at national or sub-national level. These frameworks involve different line ministries, local authorities and non-governmental bodies such as consumer advocacy groups or associations of utility professionals. In general, there are four different regulatory models: government regulation; contracts, in which regulatory regimes are specified in legal instruments; independent regulation (in decision-making, management and financing); and outsourcing (for tariff reviews, benchmarking and dispute resolution) (OECD, 2015[4]; OECD, 2009[5]).

Government tools should clearly identify regulators' functions, roles and scope of activities. This will help regulators fulfil their objectives effectively, and avoid overlap and incoherence. The OECD Survey on the Governance of Water Regulators, conducted from 2013 to 2014, sought to identify different functions exercised by 34 WWS regulators in 24 countries (OECD, 2015[4]). The survey found most regulators had four principal functions: economic regulation (tariff-setting and review of utilities' investment plans); data collection and performance monitoring related to water services; enforcement of regulations and standards; and customer engagement and protection.

Of the 34 regulators, 33 have responsibility for tariff regulation. Some of them refer to a particular methodology or criteria defined by law to carry out this role. The most widely used is the cost-plus approach, but some regulators are shifting towards setting tariffs. In some cases, however, regulators set tariffs without access to investment or business plans. Greater transparency in this area could ensure tariffs are set appropriately, and asymmetry of information could be avoided.

Service delivery

Making service delivery information publicly available could improve transparency and accountability. Monitoring service delivery performance is the second most frequent function carried out by 32 regulators. For 27 regulators, this function is combined with gathering information and data. Survey results show that a number of regulators do not make performance information, such as costs and quality of services provided, available to the public. Some withhold information partially for reasons of confidentiality, particularly concerning financial information. Countries apply several mechanisms to ensure water regulators are accountable. These include requiring regulators to report to ministers or to the legislature; making operational policies and guidance material for compliance available to the public; enacting enforcement and decision review; and giving the right to appeal the decision of regulated entities, in particular through a judicial process.

Standards setting

Regulators need to allocate human, financial and organisational resources effectively and with integrity to maintain the rule of law and create a supportive environment for investment and inclusive growth. In all, 22 regulators reported defining technical and service standards, while 25 regulators reported engaging with customers, protecting consumers and resolving disputes. The survey revealed several approaches to dispute resolution, but the most dominant was the organisation of formal meetings between representatives of the regulator and operator. The next most popular choice was legal proceedings or court sessions with a judge.

Enhancing water and wastewater services regulations in Mekong countries

In light of the typology and priorities reviewed in the previous section, this section discusses aspects of water regulation in Mekong countries, particularly in Cambodia, Lao PDR, Myanmar, Thailand and Viet Nam.

Ensuring financial sustainability in water tariff regulation

Lack of financing sources hampers scaling up of water and sanitation in rural areas. Total official financial flows of water and sanitation to developing countries have increased by 5% annually in the last decade (USD 14.3 billion in commitments on average per year in 2014-15) (OECD, 2017[6]), but financing levels are still not enough to meet the targets for drinking safe water and sanitation as climate risks are exacerbating the effects of projects on water and sanitation. While a huge amount of financing continues to flow for urban residents, most people in rural areas still lack access to basic sanitation. Expenditures for rural sanitation comprise less than 10% of total water, sanitation and hygiene (WASH) financing (WHO-UN Water, 2014[7]).

Although government budgets and expenditures for WASH are increasing, a substantial financing gap remains between budgets and plans. One critical gap is operation and maintenance (O&M), which is essential to ensure provision of sustainable and safe services. Tariffs do not cover the costs of O&M, and the quality of services and levels of coverage decline without other financing sources. Ensuring financial sustainability in water supply and sanitation in rural areas is therefore needed. For example, in Viet Nam, a limited number of households use piped water for domestic needs due to financial constraints. Many people in rural areas, especially poor households, find the connection fees (i.e. about VND 1 000 000 or USD 45 in 2013) too high for their monthly income (i.e. between VND 500 000 and VND 5 000 000) (Wilbers, Sebesvari and Renaud, 2014[8]; Vreugdenhil, Hoang and Offermans, 2012[9]).

Tariff regulation refers to several criteria related to the establishment of a tariff methodology, update of prices, supervision of tariff-setting, determination of a tariff by a consumer group and the establishment of caps on revenues or rate of return on investment. In Lao PDR, according to the 2009 water supply law, water regulators outline the tariff structures, tariff-setting process and tariff determination by end use and user category. For instance, the Vientiane state-owned water supply enterprise Nam Papa Nakhone Luang (NPNL) set a tariff of USD 0.11 per cubic metre of water (Park and Visvanathan, 2016[10]). According to their study, the NPNL tariff is still relatively low compared to the one set at USD 0.48 by the Provincial Waterworks Authority in Thailand and at USD 0.60 by the Korea Water Resources Corporation.

The low tariff set by NPNL is related to the policy that tariffs should at least cover O&M costs and be set at around 3-5% of household income. Such low tariff levels combined with poor revenue collection, high levels of non-revenue water and high operating costs, may put financial sustainability at stake. Indeed, as of late 2014, bi-annual tariff reviews and preparation for the annual performance reports of provincial water utilities, which are known as Nam Papa State Enterprises (NPSE), have become the focus of the country's water regulators – the Water Supply Regulatory Committee and the Water Supply Regulatory Office. However, tariffs are still too low to allow utilities' financial sustainability (WSP and World Bank, 2014[11]). In addition to the establishment of tariff methodology, the law also defines state responsibility to fund revenue deficits of business operators in rural areas.

Unlike in Lao PDR, regulations in Viet Nam do not clearly identify the regulator's responsibility in terms of business operators' revenues deficits. However, regulators play a more detailed role in tariff-setting. This includes the minimum pricing regulation, price calculation principles, national and regional-level pricing schemes, tariff-setting objectives, construction and development cost coverage, and financial autonomy of water supply companies.

In general, the Ministry of Finance sets a range of tariffs by considering the full-cost recovery principle, which includes the cost of water production, treatment and distribution. At the local level, tariffs are then set based on the agreement between the water supplier and the local authority. Even though tariffs cover basic operating costs, the rate is too low to support investment in asset maintenance (Trujillo, Hong and Whitley, 2015[12]; Pinto et al., 2018[13]). With such low tariffs, the Vietnamese water sector faces a challenge of financial sustainability. This is made worse by the declining tariff collection rate (especially in larger cities) and other budgetary constraints, such as the decreasing coverage rate for operating costs (World Bank, 2019[14]).

As in many developing countries, both Lao PDR and Viet Nam apply relatively low tariffs and the water sector is highly subsidised. These policies might not support effective demand management since they might discourage people from conserving water. Although increasing the tariff could possibly improve financial sustainability, political considerations often discourage this approach. In contrast to Lao PDR and Viet Nam, Myanmar and Thailand give only passing mention to tariff regulation in their legislation.

Water tariffs in Thailand are also low. For instance, the charge for raw water is based on a national tariff dating back to the 1940s, while wastewater services are free for most of the population. Adjusting these tariffs is challenging from both a technical and political point of view. The challenges include establishing customer registers and collection mechanisms, affordability issues for vulnerable customers and strategies to address the agricultural sector.

In Cambodia, the draft water supply and sanitation law addresses tariff regulation. The law will provide regulators with powers to approve or reject amendments to tariffs. The tariff itself should consider capital and recurrent costs of service provision, the efficiency of the water supply and sewerage service delivery, incentives to boost efficiency, customers' willingness to pay, equity concerns and administrative simplicity. However, the National Strategic Development Plan (NSDP) 2014-18 highlights that the water tariffs of many public waterworks remain below the level of full-cost recovery, making it difficult to cover operational and investment expenses.

Strengthening the monitoring of quality standards for drinking water

In Cambodia, the Ministry of Health issued quality standards for drinking water in 2004, which cover 12 parameters in line with standards set by the World Health Organization (WHO). The Ministry of Industry, Mines and Energy, which regulates the Phnom Penh Water Supply Authority (PPWSA) and other water supply authorities, further adopted these standards (ADB, 2012[15]). However, the groundwater, which is the main source of drinking water for many Cambodian people, is contaminated with arsenic, posing a major public health threat. Improving the quality of drinking water might be challenging for three reasons. The legal framework related to water quality standards is weak; a regular groundwater quality monitoring system is absent; and sufficient equipment and human resources for appropriate water quality management are missing (WEPA, 2015[16]).

The Ministry of Health of Lao PDR set drinking water quality targets through Decree No. 953 issued in 2003. These targets are set to achieve an agreed level of water quality in rural areas and for service providers or constructors of rural water supplies. The parameters of drinking water quality consist of the maximum allowed values of substances (e.g. iron, manganese, arsenic, fluoride, nitrate and chlorine). Other indicators include pH, turbidity, conductivity, taste and odour, which are decided through consultation with different ministries, departments and water sector agencies. In the event that mining and other industrial activities increase risk to public health, these parameters should be tested using WHO guidelines.

Language issues and accessibility to reports undermine the capacity of Lao PDR to analyse water quality. In 2014, within the Minister's Decision on Water Quality Standard for Management for Drinking and Domestic Use No. 561/MOH, the list of monitoring parameters in Lao PDR expanded from 12 to 23 indicators. The decree also mandates the National Centre of Environmental Health and Water Supply (Nam Saats) to monitor drinking water quality, sample water quality regularly and analyse samples in a laboratory. It mandates NPSEs to ensure compliance with the standard, but reports and manuscripts are mainly in the Lao language and difficult to access. This creates a barrier in understanding and analysing water quality issues in Lao PDR (Brindha, Pavelic and Sotoukee, 2019[17]).

The sole domestic source of water in Myanmar is vulnerable to pollution, and piped water is rare and not always clean. The water in Inle Lake – the country's second largest lake and sole domestic source of water – is unfit to drink (WEPA, 2015[16]). Moreover, the unavailability of a piped supply system remains a challenge, limiting access to safe drinking water. Where a piped supply system is available, water is not necessarily clean (Van Meel et al., 2014[18]). Inland surface water is generally used for domestic, irrigation and industrial activities. However, surface water is vulnerable to pollution. Inle Lake has high levels of phosphate and nitrate, and the concentration of E. coli bacteria exceeds standards, due to agricultural fertilisers and discharge of untreated waste.

Lack of both funding and qualified staff undermine the protection of water quality in Thailand. Local governments provide drinking water, while the Ministry of Health monitors compliance with national standards. The ministry regularly tests water samples from rural and urban areas, but these practices may be hampered by funding constraints, inadequate numbers of skilled graduates and recruitment practices (WHO, 2015[19]).

Better co-ordination between ministries could improve water quality in Viet Nam. The Ministry of Health sets quality standards for clean water used for daily activities, such as drinking and personal hygiene. Customers and water supply units set clean water quality standards for other activities. With respect to health, Viet Nam adapts the WHO minimum standards for drinking water quality to the country's conditions. This process involves various ministries, including Construction, and National Resources and Environment. However, while the Ministry of Health is the competent agency in setting quality standards, it is not directly involved in water sector discussions (World Bank, 2014[20]). This would suggest that better co-ordination between ministries, including Health, may help improve water quality.

The report also highlights that adequate water quality is generally not achieved at the distribution and household levels. This is largely due to quality control and monitoring that are limited to source and treatment plant outlets. In addition, reporting on drinking water quality indicators and compliance issues is still lacking. This is especially the case for distribution networks, where monitoring may not be enough to ensure that quality levels remain consistent with production quality (World Bank, 2014[20]).

Declining groundwater resources in Viet Nam are affecting water quality, requiring the government's urgent attention. For instance, in Can Tho city in the Mekong Delta, groundwater levels are falling by up to half a metre each year (Wagner, Tran and Renaud, 2012[21]; Carrard, Foster and Willetts, 2019[22]). Moreover, groundwater pollution and salinity make reliable drinking water harder to find. This is particularly the case in rural areas where the groundwater contains pesticides that exceed the levels recommended by the European Commission (Chau et al., 2015[23]; Carrard, Foster and Willetts, 2019[22]).

Ensuring law enforcement in wastewater treatment

Three Mekong countries – Cambodia, Thailand and Viet Nam – have standards for wastewater treatment and discharges. Regulators set quality standards for wastewater treatment and discharges, and then monitor compliance with these standards. In Cambodia, the Ministry of Health sets wastewater quality standards. In Thailand, the National Environment Board prescribes quality standards for ambient water. In Viet Nam, the Ministry of Natural Resources and the provincial-level People's Committees are the competent agencies.

Greater co-ordination for wastewater management among public authorities is needed in Myanmar. At the national level, different line ministries are involved in water management, covering the sectors of health, irrigation, mining, transport and industry. At the municipal level, local departments generally manage wastewater effluent standards for areas under their jurisdiction. Given the high number of public authorities involved, it is essential to strengthen co-ordination.

Wastewater is largely discharged without treatment into water sources in Myanmar. The Environmental Conservation Law approved in 2012 outlines an ambient water quality standard that encompasses surface water, marine water and groundwater in Myanmar. According to WEPA (2015[16]), water quality in Myanmar is mainly deteriorated by sewage, solid waste, and industrial and agrochemical waste. At the municipal level, particularly in rapidly industrialising cities, treatment is still complicated. Due to limited wastewater treatment facilities, wastewater discharges directly into ditches, streams, lakes and rivers (Van Meel et al., 2014[18]).

Enforcement of regulations in Cambodia is urgently needed. Inadequate institutional and legal frameworks for urban wastewater treatment remain a challenge in the country. Regulation of collection and disposal of septic effluent and sludge is reportedly inexistent. Moreover, despite legal and institutional frameworks, dumping of waste is still commonly unregulated in provincial towns (ADB, 2012[15]).

Ensuring that discharge of both untreated and treated wastewater meet the effluent standards is one of the major challenges in Thailand. The Minister of Science, Technology and Environment is habilitated to publish a notification in the Government Gazette that prescribes effluent standards. This is done with the advice of the Pollution Control Committee and is subject to approval by the National Environment Board. However, in practice, both untreated and treated wastewater discharged into the water source do not conform to the standard. On average, only 48% of establishments have obeyed the law on wastewater treatment (MONRE, 2019[24]). This has become one of the factors causing poor water quality in the downstream of Thailand's main rivers. Other challenges include O&M of wastewater treatment facilities, such as limited staff capacity, lack of funds, and tariff-setting and collection (WEPA, 2015[16]).

Most municipal and industrial wastewater is discharged untreated in Viet Nam, which could explain the poor water quality of its rivers. National legislation prescribes that individuals or organisations must be licensed to discharge wastewater into water sources. The licence should be based on standards and technical regulation on wastewater quality, the function of water sources and the capacity to receive wastewater. Construction and renovation projects, including projects of public facilities in urban areas, must have separate systems for wastewater treatment and drainage that meet technical standards. However, industries treat only 10% of industrial wastewater, despite their legal obligations (2030 WRG, 2017[25]). This might explain the poor quality of water in the downstream of Viet Nam's rivers, particularly the ones flowing through urban and industrial areas.

Addressing public service obligations and social regulation

The lack of studies on water use by community groups in Viet Nam may hamper effective planning. Viet Nam classifies water supply companies as public utilities and gives them financial autonomy to fulfil their obligations. Investment projects on construction of water supply works are required to consider socio-economic development, well-being, national defence, the protection of heritage and the natural environment as key objectives of resource exploitation. However, studies on these groups and other informal institutions are lacking, which could prevent regulators from fulfilling their social responsibilities.

Improving studies on informal institutions and considering socio-cultural practices could offer better strategies to manage water resources and provide opportunities for formal and informal institutions to interact more effectively. There are diverse socio-cultural values of water among different ethnic groups in Viet Nam. The Ha Nhi people, for example, typically leave waste besides bathing sites; this practice has resulted in increased pollution of water sources (Du et al., 2016[26]). Hygiene and sanitation services are largely region-specific, and shaped by the dominance of an ethnic group. Improper sanitation conditions, such as open pit-latrines and latrines without slabs, are found primarily in the northern mountains (10.7%), and the central highlands (9.4%). In the Mekong River Delta region, 36.5% of households use hanging latrines. Moreover, 16.5% of ethnic minority households use open pit-latrines and latrines without slabs in comparison to 1.5% of Kinh (UNICEF, 2018[27]).

Defining the standards of technical modalities and service delivery

Standards of technical modalities and level of service delivery are defined differently among countries. For instance, in Cambodia, the construction of waterworks is subject to a licence or permit. Before granting the licence or permit, the Ministry of Water Resources and Meteorology (MOWRAM) consults with local authorities and other agencies regarding water use and proposed waterworks. In addition, the law requires any person who drills or digs wells for professional or commercial purposes to submit a report to MOWRAM concerning the operation and technical specifications.

Differences in definitions could represent an obstacle to examining the urban-rural gap. In Cambodia, 58.3% of rural households have access to improved drinking water sources compared to 97.6% of households in Phnom Penh (Cambodia Socio-Economic Survey, 2017; Figure 5.1). Still, the term "improved drinking water sources" can be misleading because pollution and arsenic concentrations in groundwater are increasing. In all, 15.9% of rural households can access safely managed drinking water compared to 55.03% of urban households (JMP, 2019[28]). In this context, "safely managed drinking water" means that households can get improved water sources for drinking that are located on premises, available when needed and free from biological and chemical contamination such as arsenic (WHO-UNICEF, 2017[29]).

In Lao PDR, legislation contains provisions on environmental sustainability through its reference to policies, principles and best practices of the water infrastructure development cycle. It also mandates compliance of infrastructure with standards for construction, engineering, equipment and quality of supply. Furthermore, it specifies the roles of authorities in the technical approval of construction plans. For instance, the Ministry of Public Works and Transport manages technical approval of water supply infrastructure that serves more than 20 000 people. The provincial or municipal Public Works and Transport Department gives technical approval for water supply infrastructure serving fewer than 20 000 people.

In Myanmar, a government department, organisation or natural person needs approval of the Ministry of Transport for any construction project that could affect water resources. Conversely, in Thailand, legislation is limited to empowering the National Environment Board to seek an environmental impact assessment of projects.

Viet Nam's regulations for the water infrastructure development cycle are more detailed. They establish guidelines for water supply planning (feasibility studies) that include investigation, survey and assessment of various elements. These elements encompass the socio-economic situation and natural conditions, the status of the water supply system, the quality of surface and underground water sources, as well as the socio-economic development and the technical infrastructure system in urban areas.

Viet Nam also mandates different actors to protect the water supply system in their communities and to maintain compatible technical standards for water supply equipment. These actors include water supply units, construction management, water users and administration at all levels. While water supply units maintain the stability of water services, they co-ordinate with traffic management agencies and local administrations in case of problems. Moreover, they are responsible for comprehensive investment up to connection points. This attempts to minimise non-revenue water, leaving customers to reach individual agreements with water supply units to install meters behind connection points. Service quality at connection points, which includes water pressure, continuity and water flow for daily activities, should be compatible with the technical standards set by competent bodies. Nonetheless, focus on professional commitment to quality service remains limited (World Bank, 2019[14]). Lastly, the regulation notes the need to renovate or upgrade projects. This suggests Viet Nam can maintain quality service by minimising water supply disruptions caused by oversized infrastructure.

Identifying and preventing risk to water availability

A comprehensive approach is needed to identify and minimise risks to water availability stemming from geography, climate change and natural disasters. In Cambodia, for instance, despite the government's effort to enhance water sectors, climate risks affect national economic development and the country's ability to supply clean water to rural people. Considering that Cambodia's main agricultural produce is rice, the impact of climate change on food and agriculture is expected to get more severe. In 2018, 30.4% of the workforce was employed in agriculture, according to the World Bank World Development Indicators. That same year, agriculture, forestry and fishing contributed 22% of gross domestic product; a decline from 34.5% in 2011. Most rural households depend mainly on subsistence agriculture for their livelihoods. Rice, for example, accounts for 90% of total cultivated area and 80% of agricultural labour input. Meanwhile, disasters caused by climate emergencies such as frequent droughts hamper the supply of water for drinking and sanitation, putting the lives of millions of the most vulnerable at risk.

More efforts should be made to ensure people in rural areas have access to water. In Lao PDR, where 65% of people live in rural areas, 1.9 million persons lack access to improved water supply and 2.4 million lack access to improved sanitation service. This is due to a large disparity in access between areas close to good roads and those in remote locations (World Bank, 2014[30]). According to an annual survey, 83.9% of people had access to improved water sources for drinking water (Lao Statistics Bureau, 2018[31]). However, 78.3% of these people are in rural areas, 96.7% are in urban areas, and only 58.4% had access among the poorest quintile. In all, 73.8% of people have used improved sanitation, among whom 64.9% live in rural areas and 94.1% in urban settings. Risk identification will be useful for ensuring appropriate action and allocation of water in times of shortage.

The Netherlands is often acknowledged as a global reference for water management in terms of ensuring protection from floods and freshwater supply. The country set a sequence of priorities for freshwater supply during shortages that could serve as a reference point for the Mekong countries (Box 5.1).

Box 5.1. Sequence of priorities to tackle water shortages in the Netherlands

In the Netherlands, the central government sets the standards for the supply of national freshwater. It also sets the "sequence of priorities" to determine the allocation of freshwater to specific categories in times of shortage. The sequence is applied in exceptional circumstances.

The country defined four user categories in the sequence of priorities. Category 1, the highest priority, comprises freshwater use for safety and prevention of irreversible damage. This includes ensuring stability of flood defence structures, settling and subsidence of peat bogs and moorland, and preserving nature dependent on soil conditions. Category 2 includes utilities, such as drinking water supply and power supply. Category 3 includes small-scale high-quality use, including temporary spraying of capital-intensive crops, and process water. Category 4 includes shipping, agriculture, nature (provided that irreversible damage does not occur), industry, water recreation and lake fishing. The sequence of priorities under categories 1 and 2 cannot be adjusted, while regional water managers can establish and specify the priority uses within categories 3 and 4 (Table 5.2).

Table 5.2. Sequence of priorities for water shortage

Category 1	Category 2	Category 3	Category 4
Safety and the prevention of irreversible damage	Utilities	Small-scale high-quality use	Other (economic considerations, also in terms of nature)
1. Stability of flood defence structures	1. Drinking water supply	1. Temporary spraying of capital-intensive crops	1. Shipping
2. Setting and subsidence of peat bogs and moorland	2. Power supply	2. Process water	2. Agriculture
3. Nature dependent on soil conditions			3. Nature, as long as no irreversible damage occurs
			4. Industry
			5. Water recreation
			6. Lake fishing

Source: OECD (2014[32]), *Water Governance in the Netherlands: Fit for the Future?*, OECD Studies on Water, OECD Publishing, Paris, http://dx.doi.org/10.1787/9789264102637-en.

Providing incentives in agriculture for more efficient water use

The creation of an association for farmers could help enhance the sustainability of irrigation systems in Cambodia. In line with the principle of setting incentives for the efficient use of water resources, Cambodian legislation established the Farmers' Water User Community (FWUC). This association, which brings together all farmers with access to the same water resources, is intended to ensure an effective and sustainable management and operation of the irrigation system. Water management in Cambodia is dominated by large-scale irrigation systems that are costly, require high technical capacity and need state intervention. However, public participation remains limited in the consultation and decision-making of these large-scale projects (Sithirith, 2017[33]). The establishment of the FWUC could thus encourage collective action among Cambodian farmers to use water for irrigation in a sustainable manner. However, the same study says that, of the 525 irrigation schemes across the country, only 6.3% have an FWUC. Furthermore, only 2% of FWUC schemes are considered to be functioning well (i.e. the leaders or committee are active in the operation and management of irrigation). Moreover, less than half of FWUC farmers participate. This is due to distrust in the government among farmers, low participation rates among local government and lack of finance.

Attempts to improve water irrigation efficiency in Myanmar are hindered by many challenges. The country is promoting water conservation, in particular for agriculture, through measures such as crop pattern adjustment, water supply scheduling, land levelling, water pricing, canal lining and rehabilitation of irrigation facilities (WEPA, 2015[16]). By improving irrigation efficiency, these measures could further boost farmers' productivity. However, the irrigation systems that function well are under pressure. State-owned systems are highly subsidised and the amount charged to farmers does not cover costs. A lack of incentives to conserve water adds to the problem (Van Meel et al., 2014[18]).

Despite increasing pressures on water security, Thailand does not include improved irrigation efficiency as a role for regulators. Losses and water-use inefficiencies are considered high. This is particularly true for the agricultural sector, which accounts for over 54% of all water distributed in 2017. Moreover, growing population and industrial expansion put greater pressure on water security. Thailand may need around 5 billion cubic metres of additional water to satisfy increasing demand by 2027 (Apipattanavis, Ketpratoom and Kladkempetch, 2018[34]).

Viet Nam addresses water irrigation in its regulations, but unmonitored use of groundwater and illegal connections undermine the policy. The country has an inspection programme for water resource assessment, a plan for rational exploitation of water resources, a strategy for a water reserve and a policy to combat water pollution and unplanned exploitation. It ensures the efficient use of water resources through public consultation and approval mechanisms for investment projects involving water transfers. However, over-exploitation of unmonitored groundwater resources and illegal connections remain challenging (2030 WRG, 2017[25]). Land subsidence and saline intrusion caused by over-exploitation of resources may lead to further decline in groundwater levels and quality.

Viet Nam could consider offering incentives for farmers to increase productivity during the dry season. With rapidly increasing industrial, urban and agricultural activities, demand for water in Viet Nam continues to rise. This can be a challenge given that water sources are vulnerable to stress. Indeed, agriculture in Viet Nam consumes 81% of surface water. Therefore, the country needs to strengthen water-use efficiency. Possible measures include switching from traditional agricultural practice to crop diversification. Improving rice quality could also increase the value per unit of water used, while reducing total agricultural water demand (World Bank, 2019[14]).

Improving private sector involvement

In Lao PDR, the law on water supply outlines policies on taxation and financing sources. Both domestic and foreign investors in water supply can access loans from domestic or international financial institutions in accordance with laws and regulations. To promote investment, state land leases or concessions are exempt from fees. The WSS sector is highly dependent on external financial sources, which makes long-term planning difficult. The availability of regular financial planning and spending is still limited (SWA, 2019[35]). Increased resources from taxes would help, but additional revenues would also be needed. Boosting private investment and increasing commercial revenues offer possible options. However, poor revenue collection, high level of non-revenue water, poor functionality and high operating costs may discourage private sector involvement.

Viet Nam has policies to promote investment efficiency, but it does not provide any incentive in this regard. An exception is for the investment in water resource development aimed at reducing supply disparities between urban and marginalised populations. For instance, the government offers co-financing, as well as tax exemption, in order to increase the participation of private providers in rural areas. However, access to these incentives is limited due to complex administrative procedures, including the need for provincial governments to complete part of the application (Willetts et al., 2017[36]; Carrard et al., 2019[37]).

Even though some policies do not provide financial incentives for effective investment, they do provide support mechanisms. A water supply rotation fund, for example, enables availability of preferential financial sources for investments on water supply development in small urban centres and densely populated neighbourhoods. Other mechanisms include investment phasing and scaling of infrastructure to be suitable for up to five years from the date of commission. They also require investment plans or feasibility studies to consider life cycle costs.

Private sector involvement in publicly financed infrastructure projects remains limited. Most private sector participation is concentrated in projects funded by international financial institutions (2030 WRG, 2017[25]). Moreover, several issues discourage the international private sector from investing in the national WWS sector. These include inadequate loan security and lack of guaranteed minimum returns, standard contracts and common procedures. Tackling these issues would help increase both national and international private sector participation.

Promoting innovative technologies through public-private partnership

Regulatory bodies can provide incentives or specific schemes to promote innovative technologies. For instance, in Cambodia, the government grants rewards or incentives for research and development (R&D) of new technologies and installations of modern equipment that aim to reduce waste, improve water quality and increase water-use efficiency.

Viet Nam uses investment and other mechanisms to encourage R&D and to apply technologies. Notably, this covers efficient water resource development, wastewater recycling, saline and brackish water transformation, efficient rainwater collection and use, artificial groundwater supply, source rehabilitation and management of externalities. Declining water quality and increasing water demand have prompted Viet Nam to introduce appropriate technology to improve water quality and to manage water supply sustainably. The *Korea Smart Water Management* (K-SWM) initiative, for example, aims to improve water management by integrating information and communication technology (Box 5.2).

Box 5.2. Korea Smart Water Management

Driven by growing uncertainty over future water availability and demand, and risks of floods and water scarcity due to climate change, the Korean Water Resources Corporation, or K-water, has developed Smart Water Management (SWM). By integrating information and communication technology (ICT), the SWM is intended to produce and use large volumes of data in real time. This would support water resources management at different scales, such as data management, flood prevention, detection of leakage and promotion of water-use efficiency by households.

Two major elements of K-SWM are the integrated dam management and the Smart City water project.

Integrated dam management combines water infrastructure and ICT. It anticipates water demand and availability in real time, allowing better risk management of floods and droughts. ICT also enables the provision of real-time data on water use, expected rainfalls and available room in reservoirs, making it easier to manage dams and water bodies.

Through ICT, the Smart City water project provides consumers with instant and reliable information on water use, and the quality and quantity of water supply. Such mechanisms may further help detect leakage and encourage tap water drinking. As water suppliers in Korea need to replace ageing infrastructure, additional financing sources are needed. Minimising non-revenue water by reducing leakage and increasing consumption, particularly for drinking purposes, provides a clear way to increase revenues from water tariffs, while keeping prices low. While K-water leads SWM, other water suppliers could supply ICT integration to help detect leakage and inform consumers about water quality as need arises from cities and households.

Several cities are piloting applications for domestic water users, including smart water meters that monitor water quality in real time. As users see value in improved service, they have more trust in the system and are more willing to drink tap water. Despite these benefits, K-SWM has significant initial transaction costs, especially stemming from the time spent by K-water staff to promote and roll out the project in pilot cities. In addition, local governments must pay for smart water meters. Thus, for K-SWM to be rolled out beyond pilot cities, the business model should allow recouping these costs by increasing efficiency or earning revenue.

The cost of too much, too little or too polluted water is a global issue that SWM could help minimise. As such, there is potential demand for SWM abroad. However, SWM relies extensively on ICT to maintain and operate the system. This might work in the Korean context, but could be difficult to deploy in developing countries. As a result, the potential diffusion of SWM abroad should take into account the target countries' capacity to adapt and adjust innovation to local conditions.

Source: OECD (2017[6]), *Enhancing Water Use Efficiency in Korea: Policy Issues and Recommendations*, OECD Studies on Water, OECD Publishing, Paris.

The legislation also considers the modernisation and manufacture of water supply equipment. For instance, big cities such as Hanoi, Hai Phong and Ho Chi Minh City, as well as dynamic urban areas and industrial parks, apply modern technologies to the water supply system. In addition, the policy highlights the full use of domestic equipment, facilities and supplies to reduce investment cost, as well as use of synchronised technical equipment to simplify replacement.

In Thailand, the Metropolitan Waterworks Authority (MWA) has supported innovation by promoting water saving devices and establishing a mobile application for consumers and software that helps detect leaky pipes (MWA, 2018[38]). Conversely, regulations in Lao PDR and Myanmar put little focus on promoting innovative technologies.

Since applying innovative technology may require large amounts of investment, public-private partnerships could be one solution. These could support water start-ups and accelerate innovation (Box 5.3).

Box 5.3. Water Innovation Accelerator

Founded in 2012, the Water Innovation Accelerator (WIN) is a virtual network-centred incubator model in Sweden. It aims to fast track water-related innovations through assistance, financing and access to market for small and medium-sized enterprises (SMEs). The network is made up of the private sector (SMEs and large corporations), the public sector (municipalities and public utilities) and academia (universities and research institutes). Participating innovation companies engage particularly in innovative solutions for drinking water, wastewater, infrastructure, measurements and energy. Through networking, these companies can get early feedback directly from the market. This allows them to adjust their focus and make the most of innovation to reach their full potential. As a non-profit organisation, WIN receives funding mainly from membership fees of partner organisations and the Swedish Agency for Economic and Regional Growth.

WIN organises regular meetings, allowing both innovation companies and other partners to share their experience and insights. The meetings also serve as matchmaking activities where members can find potential business models for commercialising their innovations. The matchmaking between participants is done through a "mingle map" developed by WIN management. Within the mingle map, a circle is drawn by dots, in which each dot represents participating organisations (Figure 5.1). Lines, which represent potential business opportunities identified by the WIN team, connect these dots. In general, at least two lines connect each organisation. During meetings, participants use the map to identify business opportunities that have been suggested to them.

Figure 5.1. Illustration of mingle map

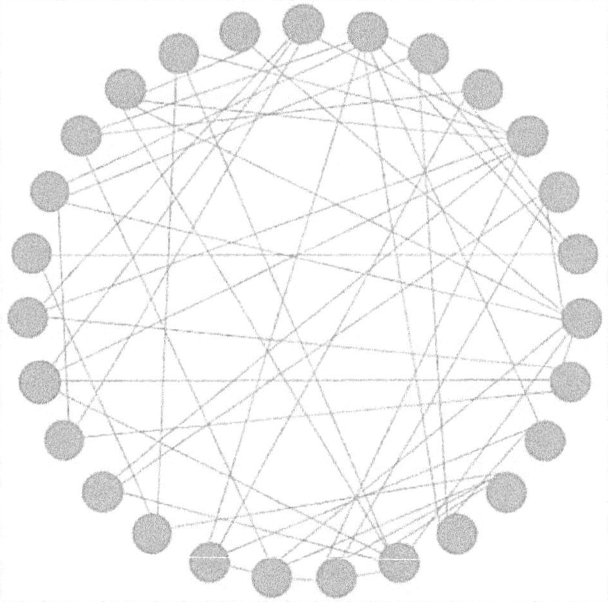

Source: OECD Development Centre adapted from Gabrielsson et al. (2018[39]).

Gabrielsson et al. (2018[39]) show that most WIN participants find several value-added elements to develop their business. In less than two years, WIN has helped several SMEs to grow by giving them access to risk capital, test beds and a better understanding of solutions needed by the municipal or by multinational companies to develop their business (Gabrielsson et al., 2018[39]). The study also found that benefits for SMEs depend on the phase of the innovation process they are at. For instance, the acceleration process worked better for SMEs at the commercialisation stage than for those at an earlier stage of innovation. This suggests that WIN's network-centred approach may be an effective way to support development and market uptake of water innovations.

Facilitating initiatives to reduce water demand

Regulators promote demand management through incentives or specific schemes to reduce water demand. Thailand has launched different activities targeted to students and the wider public. For instance, within the school environment, the Water Conservation Camp raises awareness of the value of water and water conservation among students in two river basin areas in Nonthaburi province (MWA, 2018[38]).

In Viet Nam, water stress or even severe water stress is expected in five river basins by 2030 (2030 WRG, 2017[25]), making it vital to reduce water demand. Lessening the water stress level from "severe" to "low" during the dry season by 2030 requires reducing annual demand by 2.5 billion cubic metres from the Mekong Basin alone (2030 WRG, 2017[25]). Reducing water demand from the remaining basins, which serve agricultural, industrial and municipal purposes, is also necessary. Interventions in each sector, or even a mix of interventions, may offer a path to achieve the required target.

Low awareness of protecting water resources and lack of commitment in reducing water use are examples of demand management challenges. In the Vietnamese society, water is perceived as a "limitless God-given resource" (Du et al., 2016[26]). Such attitudes are common primarily in urban areas, which have a high incidence of littering in public spaces and waterways. Indeed, the law on water resources highlights policies on communication and education, emphasising measures to protect water resources and to conserve water under the guidance of central and local governments. In this case, co-ordination between state agencies, mass-media agencies, and education and training institutions is essential. Moreover, political organisations, in co-ordination with state agencies in charge of water resources, may mobilise people to participate in water resource protection, as well as to monitor the protection and exploitation of water resources.

Better water demand management could offer several benefits. If water conservation can defer development of a new water source, the government could allocate the saved funds for other urgent matters. Demand management could also promote efficient use of water. From the customers' side, reducing water consumption could lower water bills if charges are variable, depending on consumption rather than fixed (McIntosh, 2014[40]). Cambodia, Lao PDR and Myanmar, however, seem to be lagging behind in terms of demand management.

Analysing investment plans of water utilities

Information related to analysing water utilities' investment plans or business plans seems to be lacking in Cambodia, Lao PDR, Myanmar and Thailand. On the contrary, in Viet Nam, investment in water supply units must comply with approved construction plans and include public consultation with the relevant communities to develop feasibility studies. This is in line with the principles of stability, safety, and resiliency, as well as the principle of economic and financial viability in the Asia-Pacific Economic Co-operation Guidebook on Quality of Water Infrastructure and Development. Viet Nam also requires water supply units to seek approval from People's Committees on their annual and long-term water supply development plans in the respective service areas. Once these plans are approved, the units remain responsible for investments in distribution networks and customer-level connection. However, the high level of decentralisation may become a challenge due to different levels of competence in project development and implementation, as well as possible conflicts of interest (World Bank, 2019[14]).

Improving information gathering and data collection

Countries in the Mekong region face a difficulty in obtaining data from water utility records. Lack of data becomes an issue, for example, in cases of unmetered connections or unreliable meter readings (Nauges and Whittington, 2009[41]). When households are connected to unmetered piped-water networks, water utilities and households themselves struggle to obtain estimates of the volume of water used. Where connections are metered, readings can also sometimes be unreliable. For instance, with intermittent water supply, air that enters the pipes can be registered as water, providing inaccurate readings. Low water tariffs in many developing countries exacerbate this problem, giving little incentive for water utilities to improve the O&M of water meters.

Cambodia, Lao PDR and Viet Nam collect data from operators and research the market to identify trends and potential risks. Cambodia requires national, provincial and municipal institutions in the WWS sector to submit data on quantity, quality and other relevant information to MOWRAM. Data are freely available to all government agencies and the public, except for those classified as confidential. MOWRAM may charge for data requested for commercial purposes. In Lao PDR, legislation outlines the creation of the National Water Supply Data and Information System. The database aims to support the development, monitoring, assessment of implementation of policies, strategic plans and water supply operations.

Viet Nam has more detailed water resource management policies. These refer to investments on water resource observation; a surveillance, information and database system; information gathering on lists of river basins and water sources; information sharing with organisations and individuals; a water resource survey and master plan survey; and requirements for a water resource inventory and reporting every five years. Viet Nam charges organisations and individuals for their use of information on water resources. This policy might become a barrier for those willing to use the data, as well as limit information and data sharing among stakeholders.

In Cambodia and Myanmar, data comparability and accessibility issues remain challenging. In Cambodia, datasets on water supply and sanitation are incompatible (ADB, 2012[15]). This is due to infrequent data collection, differences in definitions, lack of co-ordination between agencies and lack of consensus on service indicators. In Myanmar, many data are lacking, and those available are difficult to access.

Developing capacity in licensing of water operators

In keeping with the NSDP 2014-18, the Cambodian Ministry of Industry and Handicraft licenses private water operators. As of 2015, Cambodia had about 300 water operators, of which only 147 are licensed. In response, the urban water supply sector has prioritised developing the capacities of the relevant agency in licensing and bringing all unlicensed operators under its supervision (WSP and World Bank, 2015[42]). In Lao PDR, the legislation defines requirements to establish water supply enterprises. It also outlines an investment mechanism policy and allocation of responsibility for construction approval among vertical actors. These include provincial and municipal jurisdictions, and the Ministry of Public Works and Transport.

In Viet Nam, a water supply unit may invest in or invite investment for activities associated with water supply. For areas without water supply units, legal provisions for bidding and specific conditions of each community dictate the criteria for selection of water supply units for investment.

Depending on the location of the projects, different actors select the water supply units in Viet Nam. For instance, the Ministry of Construction selects water supply units for urban centres or industrial parks needing water supply works of inter-provincial scale. Meanwhile, the Ministry of Agriculture and Rural Development selects such units for rural areas. The legislation also defines the conditions for consultancy units to elaborate water resource master plans, as well as the conditions for the transfer of rights to water supply service businesses. In Myanmar and Thailand, granting or approving licences to operate water systems is barely mentioned in legislation or policy.

Strengthening the supervision of contracts with utilities and private actors

Legislation in both Lao PDR and Viet Nam covers the supervision of contracts with utilities and private actors. Lao PDR specifies rights and obligations of concessionaires, as well as conditions for length and termination of contracts. Its legislation also requires water supply service providers to install sanitation infrastructure. It is understood that fire departments can use water for free. Similarly, the Vietnamese legislation defines rights and obligations of both water supply units and customers. In this way, it aims to meet the multi-dimensional needs of stakeholders. These can include protecting both parties against concerns such as market abuse, damage from externalities like pollution and conflicting information from different sources. These regulations, which affect both local authorities and water supply units, have not been adequately enforced (World Bank, 2019[14]). In addition, quality assurance services for local authorities and consumer protection have not been implemented. Consequently, all parties might be exposed to risk. For all these reasons, the regulations fall short on providing investment incentives. The legislation also provides details on the supervision of contracts between private actors and end users. For instance, water supply units connect customers through distribution networks to balance water-use demands, and charge them a water-use fee.

Monitoring utilities' financing activities

While supervision of contracts with utilities or private actors can be identified within Viet Nam's legislation, supervision of utilities' financing activities seems to be lacking in this country. This function, which consists of monitoring the financial schemes of water utilities, can be identified in Lao PDR and Thailand. Lao PDR authorises the establishment of a fund to maintain, improve and develop the water supply infrastructure. The Water Supply Development Fund is financed through the state budget and assistance from domestic or foreign individuals and organisations, including service providers. In addition, the legislation defines policies on profit taxes, investors' duties, access to sources of funds and exemption of fees on state land leases or concessions in accordance with the law on investment promotion. In Thailand, in accordance with the National Environmental Quality Act, the Environment Fund finances several activities related to water quality management. Interest from fixed deposits must be spent on Fund activities and not remitted to the Treasury. In addition, legislation defines the Fund's responsibilities for different activities related to water quality management.

Increasing public participation

Regulators communicate decisions and other issues to the public, and may consult them regularly. For instance, in Cambodia, the PPWSA launches campaigns and maintains contact with communities to disseminate information related to services, such as procedures to obtain new connections; information related to water tariffs, subsidies, penalties for illegal water connection, non-payment of bills and water quality (Das et al., 2010[43]).

In Viet Nam, the Ministry of Construction encourages people and communities to help manage and oversee water supply activities. The legislation requires public consultation and approval of projects related to water resource exploitation and discharge of wastewater into water sources. Investment projects that involve water transfer are also subject to consultation with competent authorities, such as the People's Committees and river basin organisations. In practice, however, civil society, research institutions and local communities have limited participation in the decision-making process (Grafton et al., 2019[44]). This might be due to factors such as lack of implementation guidelines and absence of targeted resources.

While customer engagement in Viet Nam focuses on water supply-related activities, Thai legislation emphasises individual rights and duties, as well as involvement of non-governmental bodies in environmental protection. However, the lack of understanding of wastewater problems and environmental protection among Thai communities are barriers to public participation (WEPA, 2015[16]). In Thailand, the MWA established the "Quality Water for Quality Life" project to build networks and get customer feedback. The initiative consists mainly of events where participants can learn about services related to plumbing, inspection and leakage repair, as well as the MWA mobile application and consumer satisfaction (MWA, 2018[38]). There is little mention of customer engagement within the legislation or policies of Lao PDR and Myanmar.

Managing dispute resolution and consumer protection

In Cambodia, the PPWSA receives consumer complaints related to issues such as water consumption, connection, metering and leakage. They are reported to relevant units and recorded by the data entry department (Das et al., 2010[43]).

In Lao PDR, service users can complain to authorities about either the quality or quantity of the water supply. Consumers may also receive compensation for losses resulting from water supply services as defined by law. Dispute resolution includes mediation or conciliation, administrative settlement, arbitration, court judgement and international charter resolution.

In Thailand, individuals have the right to compensation against damage from pollution. Citizens also have the right and duty to report on offenders if they witness any violation of laws related to pollution control or conservation of natural resources.

Viet Nam's legislation stipulates more detailed rights for consumers. Legislation covers errors and damage compensation, water charge payments, water measuring equipment and settlement of complaints and reports of illegal acts. For instance, with regard to water charge payment, authorities may compensate consumers for excessive charges by water supply units. Consumers may also complain about inaccurate measurement and be compensated for inspection of equipment. One particular challenge related to compensation in Viet Nam's water sector industry includes the absence of capacity and technical knowledge in quantifying losses (Grafton et al., 2019[44]).

Addressing water sector challenges through capacity building

Regulators provide advice and advocacy for reforming and improving the regulatory framework. However, among the Mekong countries, Viet Nam provides details on its policy. Three examples from the policy, established in 1998, relate to governance reform, financial policy renewal and human resource development.

First, governance reform targets restructuring of inappropriate organisations at central and local levels, and raises the role of local authorities at all levels in water supply management. Nonetheless, highly decentralised management might become a challenge once actors work together less often. The dual supervisory roles of central agencies and provincial People's Committees, alongside unclear reporting mechanisms, might also reduce water governance efficiency (Grafton et al., 2019[44]).

Second, financial policy renewal outlines the mobilisation of multi-sectoral finance, tariff-setting for financial autonomy and cost coverage for wastewater drainage in urban areas.

Third, human resource development covers building capacity of all personnel in the water supply sector from management to technicians. It also encourages contributions from non-resident Vietnamese experts. However, the number of qualified staff in water resources management, particularly within the Ministry of Natural Resources and Environment (MONRE), remains limited. MONRE's 2010 staff survey revealed that water sector experts account for only 0.4% of personnel (Du et al., 2016[26]). This includes staff skilled in specialised water management software. Given the small proportion of qualified staff in the water sector, the government must improve its human resources capacity to achieve its water-related goals and responsibilities. Improving human resources capacity could be done, among others, through the establishment of training centres. In Tokyo, Japan, for example, the Bureau of Waterworks established the largest waterworks training institution in the country (Box 5.4).

Box 5.4. Tokyo Bureau of Waterworks Training and Technical Development Centre

The Bureau of Waterworks, Tokyo [Japan] Metropolitan Government, created the Training and Development Centre in April 2005 – the largest centre in the country for training, and research and development (R&D) functions. The centre provides various facilities for experience-based training, including a simulation of water pipe laying sites. It allows trainees at the Bureau, other water utilities in Japan and overseas visitors to acquire on-site waterworks techniques and capabilities.

The Tokyo Waterworks prepares annual training programmes for staff. In addition to training and upskilling programmes, the Bureau ensures that accumulated knowledge is passed down effectively among staff. In July 2008, a system for experts was launched to securely disseminate information on the waterworks techniques accumulated to date. In this system, staff members with particularly high skills and extensive experience are certified as experts. These experts share their own experience and knowledge in documents, videos and other materials to be used by other staff. They are also expected to guide and advise other staff members from different work sites.

A knowledge management system has also been established by consolidating and using technical information to master the waterworks techniques (Figure 5.2). As part of this management system, a knowledge bank was developed and started operating in April 2007. The accumulated knowledge and data are stored in a database.

The Bureau of Waterworks conducts R&D in a wide range of areas, including leakage detection equipment and water meters, corrosion resistance of service/distribution pipes and water treatment technology. Additionally, it conducts collaborative research with private companies and universities to introduce advanced technologies and know-how. These achievements are used for various operations within the Bureau, and also help improve the technological capability of water utilities across the country.

Figure 5.2. Tokyo Waterworks Knowledge Management System

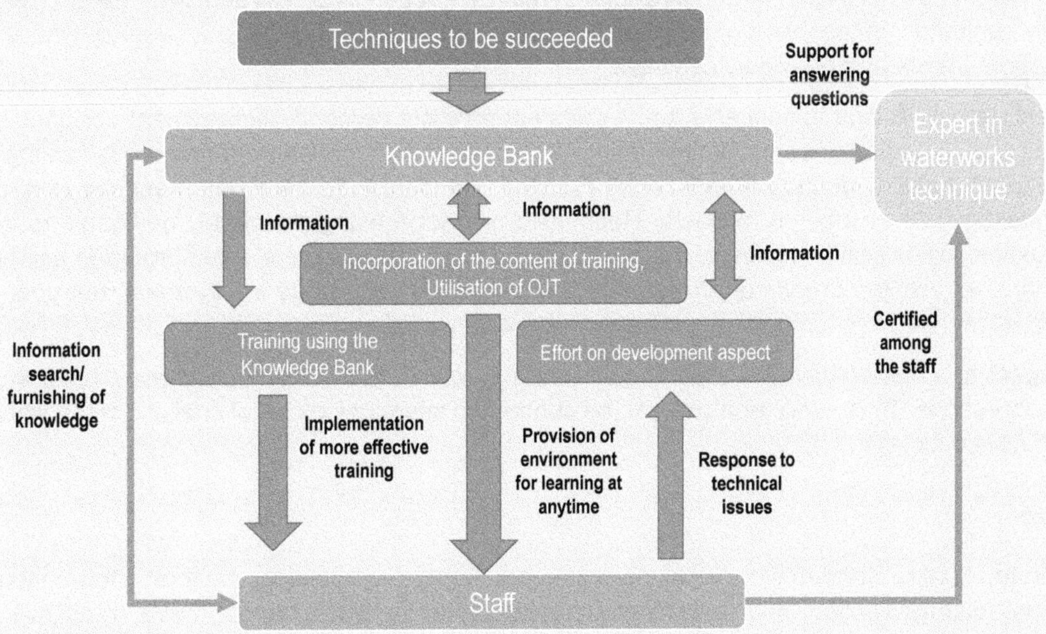

Note: OJT = On-the-job training.
Source: (Bureau of Waterworks Tokyo Metropolitan Government, n.d.[45]), *Water Supply in Tokyo*, https://www.waterworks.metro.tokyo.jp/eng/business/supply/ (accessed on 16 March 2020).

Water regulation summaries by country

Cambodia

In Cambodia, rural water systems lag behind those of Phnom Penh. Generally, the regulation of water systems is incomplete. Water tariffs are too low to support full cost-recovery of water system operations. A shortage of physical and human capital impairs proper management of drinking water sources, which leads to contamination, especially in rural areas. Weak enforcement undercuts already weak laws pertaining to water treatment. Meanwhile, weak institutions limit the ability of affected customers to seek recourse. Fewer than half of all private water supply operators are licensed.

Standard definitions are essential to improve access. Differences in definitions of terms and policies among jurisdictions have contributed to a drinking water access gap. Nearly all residents of Phnom Penh have drinking water piped into their dwellings. Elsewhere, less than 60% of residents have piped water, despite strong centralisation of waterworks planning and permits by MOWRAM. The variability of definitions also results in data inconsistencies, making any research difficult or suspect. On a positive note, data are centralised in one agency.

The government provides R&D grants for water conservation technologies. For those efforts to reach their full potential, Cambodia must promote water demand management initiatives, such as education programmes and FWUC. However, the credibility of institutions remains a barrier.

Lao PDR

Water regulations are well-defined in Lao PDR. Regulations on tariffs, drinking water quality, infrastructure development, and supervision of private water provision contracts, and utility financing activities exist in federal legislation or ministry decrees. Roles of ministries and the levels of government are well-delineated, allowing for co-operation without wasteful duplication. A robust National Data and Information System supports these functions. Water consumers enjoy considerable protection. Tariffs are well-stratified, but could be increased in all areas. Water supplier contracts are supervised, and suppliers are also responsible for supply sanitation. In the event of disputes, customers can file complaints to an agency where avenues for resolution are strong and widely available.

In contrast, Lao PDR lags in conservation. It does not promote demand management nor does it provide incentives for R&D into conservation technologies. Monitoring of service performance is lacking, and the term itself is not clearly defined. If monitoring results in an inability to detect and respond to issues such as pipe leakage, water may go to waste. Responsibilities for funding are clearly delegated to the Water Supply Development Fund. However, much of the funding for both potable water provision and sanitation is external. Tax and fee breaks on investment and operation encourage involvement, but poor revenue collection, along with high operating costs deter external investment.

With respect to water quality, the reporting structure is robust. However, reports are written in Lao and highly inaccessible. Thus, while analysis can be conducted internally, external analysis of the water quality of Lao PDR is difficult.

Myanmar

In Myanmar, quality standards for drinking water are poor, and drinking water is often contaminated. Institutional disorganisation and insufficient infrastructure in urban areas make it difficult to treat wastewater. In terms of conservation, government efforts are largely futile. State-owned irrigation systems do not recover costs, making maintenance or upgrades difficult. On a positive note, construction projects that may impact water resources require Ministry of Transport approval. Data and service monitoring is limited in scope, depth, access or a combination thereof. Notably, of all the Mekong countries surveyed, Myanmar has the most fields missing from its table (see Annex Table 5.A.3).

Thailand

Thailand's legislation for water regulation is either weak or ignored. Tariffs have remained mostly unchanged since the 1940s and are far below the amount required to cover operational costs. Drinking water quality is subject to national standards, and testing is both extensive and reliable. There are areas for improvement, but more skilled labour is needed in these areas. Water contamination is common due to regulations being ignored. Likewise, environmental impact studies of construction projects are only undertaken upon request, putting water supplies at further risk of contamination.

Water demand management is compulsory in the education system. The MWA promotes the production of devices and services to control demand, but it does not seem to encourage changes in behaviour nor the adoption of these technologies.

The "Quality Water for Quality Life" initiative allows people to access information on both do-it-yourself and government repairs, as well as to provide user feedback. The initiative publicises rights and duties of environmental protection, but more public education is needed to make them understood. As of now, they are mostly ignored. Service delivery performance does not appear to be monitored in Thailand either, as is common in most Mekong countries. Customers have the right to seek compensation for damages caused by pollution and to report environmental law offenders. In contrast, they do not seem to provide a mechanism for compensation relating to service failures.

From a financial perspective, the Environmental Fund is responsible for water management. Strict criteria must be met to access money from the Fund. However, efforts should be made to enact incentives for further foreign investment in the Thai water sector.

Thailand appears to have appropriate water regulation given its legislative challenges. Stricter enforcement of legislation and devising foreign investment opportunities would allow Thailand to access foregone potential in that sector.

Viet Nam

Viet Nam possesses robust water regulations, in general. While its specific policies may not be applicable to every country, the depth and scope of Viet Nam's regulations could be emulated. To do this, improved enforcement and human capital is critical.

Tariff regulations are detailed, and water supply companies have financial autonomy. However, as with every other Mekong country for which tariff data are available, tariff schedules fail to provide full cost recovery. The Ministry of Health sets quality standards for drinking water. Licensing and quality standards are in place for wastewater treatment, but most wastewater flows into streams untreated, harming downstream water quality. Socio-cultural differences among ethnic and religious groups hamper water quality preservation efforts in Viet Nam. The population does not universally understand the value of water and sanitation practices. Formal studies are required to determine the exact differences and how to successfully change behaviour.

Service quality standards are well defined, and any water infrastructure expansion requires feasibility studies. However, there are deficiencies in monitoring. In keeping with standards, maintenance is a collective effort and the country encourages routine renovation of systems. Individual water suppliers are responsible for metering. Consumers can seek compensation for overcharging, but technology to identify this practice is lacking. This harms both conservation efforts and consumers. Water conservation policies exist, but compliance is challenging. Many Vietnamese view water as a limitless resource bestowed upon them by God. Consequently, there is little concern for demand management. Policies exist, but illegal connections to water sources are common and groundwater contamination remains an ongoing issue. Rice, the main crop grown in Viet Nam, is extremely water-intensive, so authorities should pursue incentives to control agricultural water use. Legislation promotes the development of technologies to address high water demand and the declining quality of service. Licensing of water operators is mainly local, leading to system variations. Standardisation of infrastructure parts would improve maintenance in terms of both shorter downtimes and lower costs. Reducing or eliminating regulatory duplication would represent a significant step towards improved efficiency.

As a measure of efficiency, all investments in water infrastructure must be valid for five years after the date of their commissioning. A potential avenue for investment growth is expansion of investment incentives beyond projects to close the urban-rural gap. Water supply investments must comply with approved construction plans, and are subject to feasibility studies and public consultation before approval. In practice, public consultation is limited due to lack of interest. Improved enforcement of legitimate rights and obligations for both suppliers and consumers would encourage investment.

Conclusion

Water and wastewater regulators are usually part of a broad regulatory framework at national or sub-national level. These involve different line ministries, local authorities and non-governmental bodies such as consumer advocacy groups or associations of utilities. Out of 19 types of regulatory functions, all Mekong countries define technical or industry and service standards by type of function. However, they all seem to lack services for monitoring performance and managing audits on utilities.

In general, the five countries may need to address tariffs (which are too low to cover O&M), lack of data and limited human resource capacity. This suggests there is scope to improve regulation of the WWS sector in Mekong countries. Such reform could embrace the efforts of government, communities and societies to create a sense of ownership in the positive impacts of projects and policy tools. Complex challenges such as governance and financial sustainability are found throughout the Mekong region with respect to accessing water infrastructure. Universal access to drinking safe water, sanitation and hygiene can provide benefits across sectors, including health, well-being, economy and the environment.

References

2030 WRG (2017), *Vietnam – Hydro-Economic Framework for Assessing Water Sector Challenges*, 2030 Water Resources Group, Washington, DC, http://www.2030wrg.org/wp-content/uploads/2017/08/Vietnam-Hydro-Economic-Framework.pdf. [25]

ADB (2012), *Cambodia: Water Supply and Sanitation Sector Assessment, Strategy, and Road Map*, Asian Development Bank, Mandaluyoung, http://www.adb.org/sites/default/files/institutional-document/33593/files/cam-water-supply-sanitation-sector-assessment.pdf. [15]

Apipattanavis, S., S. Ketpratoom and P. Kladkempetch (2018), "Water Management in Thailand", *Irrigation and Drainage*, Vol. 67/1, pp. 113-117, http://dx.doi.org/10.1002/ird.2207. [34]

Brindha, K., P. Pavelic and T. Sotoukee (2019), "Environmental assessment of water and soil quality in the Vientiane Plain, Lao PDR", *Groundwater for Sustainable Development*, Vol. 8, pp. 24-30, http://dx.doi.org/10.1016/j.gsd.2018.08.005. [17]

Bureau of Waterworks Tokyo Metropolitan Government (n.d.), *Water Supply in Tokyo*, https://www.waterworks.metro.tokyo.jp/eng/business/supply/ (accessed on 16 March 2020). [45]

Carrard, N., T. Foster and J. Willetts (2019), "Groundwater as a Source of Drinking Water in Southeast Asia and the Pacific: A Multi-Country Review of Current Reliance and Resource Concerns", *Water*, Vol. 11/8, p. 1605, http://dx.doi.org/10.3390/w11081605. [22]

Carrard, N. et al. (2019), "Are piped water services reaching poor households? Empirical evidence from rural Viet Nam", *Water Research*, Vol. 153, pp. 239-250, http://dx.doi.org/10.1016/j.watres.2019.01.026. [37]

Chau, N. et al. (2015), "Pesticide pollution of multiple drinking water sources in the Mekong Delta, Vietnam: evidence from two provinces", *Environmental Science and Pollution Research*, Vol. 22/12, pp. 9042-9058, http://dx.doi.org/10.1007/s11356-014-4034-x. [23]

Das, B. et al. (2010), *Sharing the Reform Process, Mekong Water Dialogue*, International Union for Conservation of Nature and Natural Resources, Gland, https://ppwsa.com.kh/en/index.php?page=sharingthereformprocess. [43]

Du, T. et al. (2016), "Water governance in a changing era: Perspectives on Vietnam", in *Water Governance Dynamics in the Mekong Region*, Strategic Information and Research Development Centre, Selangor, http://www.researchgate.net/publication/314155865_Water_Governance_in_a_Changing_Era_Perspectives_on_Vietnam. [26]

Gabrielsson, J. et al. (2018), "Promoting water-related innovation through networked acceleration: Insights from the Water Innovation Accelerator", *Journal of Cleaner Production*, Vol. 171, pp. S130-S139, http://dx.doi.org/10.1016/j.jclepro.2016.07.101. [39]

Grafton, R. et al. (2019), "The Water Governance Reform Framework: Overview and Applications to Australia, Mexico, Tanzania, U.S.A and Vietnam", *Water*, Vol. 11/1, p. 137, http://dx.doi.org/10.3390/w11010137. [44]

JMP (2019), *WHO/UNICEF Joint Monitoring Programme (database)*, https://washdata.org/data/household#!/dashboard/new (accessed on 13 May 2020). [28]

Lao Statistics Bureau (2018), *Lao Social Indicator Survey II 2017, Survey Findings Report*, Vientiane, Lao PDR: Lao Statistics Bureau and UNICEF, https://washdata.org/sites/default/files/documents/reports/2018-08/Lao-Social-Indicator-Survey-Lsis-II-2017.pdf. [31]

McIntosh, A. (2014), *Urban Water Supply and Sanitation in Southeast Asia: A Guide to Good Practice*, Asian Development Bank, Mandaluyong, https://think-asia.org/handle/11540/2501. [40]

MONRE (2019), ""Progress of Water Environment Governance in Thailand"", Ministry of Natural Resources and Environment, http://wepa-db.net/3rd/en/meeting/20190222/pdf/D2_S3_Thailand.pdf. [24]

MWA (2018), *Annual Report 2018*, Metropolitan Waterworks Authority, Bangkok, http://www.mwa.co.th/mobile/download/Annual_Report_2561_eng.pdf. [38]

Nauges, C. and D. Whittington (2009), "Estimation of water demand in developing countries: An overview", *The World Bank Research Observer*, World Bank, Washington, DC, pp. 263-294, https://documents.worldbank.org/en/publication/documents-reports/documentdetail/490481468346446277/estimation-of-water-demand-in-developing-countries-an-overview. [41]

OECD (2020), *Economic Outlook for Southeast Asia, China and India 2020 – Update: Meeting the Challenges of COVID-19*, OECD Publishing, Paris, https://dx.doi.org/10.1787/e8c90b68-en. [1]

OECD (2017), *Enhancing Water Use Efficiency in Korea: Policy Issues and Recommendations*, OECD Studies on Water, OECD Publishing, Paris, https://dx.doi.org/10.1787/9789264281707-en. [6]

OECD (2015), *The Governance of Water Regulators*, OECD Studies on Water, OECD Publishing, Paris, https://dx.doi.org/10.1787/9789264231092-en. [4]

OECD (2014), *Water Governance in the Netherlands: Fit for the Future?*, OECD Studies on Water, OECD Publishing, Paris, https://dx.doi.org/10.1787/9789264102637-en. [32]

OECD (2009), *Private Sector Participation in Water Infrastructure: OECD Checklist for Public Action*, OECD Studies on Water, OECD Publishing, Paris, https://dx.doi.org/10.1787/9789264059221-en. [5]

Oxford Economics and Global Infrastructure Hub (2017), *Global Infrastructure Outlook*. [2]

Park, D. and C. Visvanathan (2016), "Technology development trajectory for drinking water treatment: a comparative study between South Korea, Thailand, and Lao PDR", *Journal of Water Supply: Research and Technology-Aqua*, Vol. 65/5, pp. 417-430, http://dx.doi.org/10.2166/aqua.2016.110. [10]

Pinto, F. et al. (2018), "Contributing to water security through water tariffs: some guidelines for implementation mechanisms", *Journal of Water, Sanitation and Hygiene for Development*, Vol. 8/4, pp. 730-739, http://dx.doi.org/10.2166/washdev.2018.015. [13]

Sithirith, M. (2017), "Water Governance in Cambodia: From Centralized Water Governance to Farmer Water User Community", *Resources*, Vol. 6/3, p. 44, http://dx.doi.org/10.3390/resources6030044. [33]

SWA (2019), "The Laos Country Brief", *Sector Ministers' Meeting 2019*, Sanitation and Water for All, http://sanitationandwaterforall.org/wp-content/uploads/download-manager-files/Laos%20Country%20Brief.pdf. [35]

Trujillo, N., V. Hong and S. Whitley (2015), "Mapping current incentives and investment in Viet Nam's water and sanitation sector: Informing private climate finance", Working Paper, No. 417, Overseas Development Institute, London, https://www.odi.org/sites/odi.org.uk/files/odi-assets/publications-opinion-files/9642.pdf. [12]

UNESCO WWAP (United Nations World Water Assessment Programme) (2017), *The United Nations World Water Development Report 2017. Wastewater: The Untapped Resource*, Paris, UNESCO, https://unesdoc.unesco.org/ark:/48223/pf0000247153. [3]

UNICEF (2018), *Evaluation of UNICEF Viet Nam Rural Sanitation and Hygiene Programme (RSHP) 2012-2016*, https://www.unicef.org/evaldatabase/files/Evaluation_of_UNICEF_VN_Rual_Sanitation_and_Hygiene_Programme_2012-2016_Vietnam_2018-003.pdf. [27]

Van Meel, P. et al. (2014), *Myanmar IWRM Strategic Study: Research and Analysis, Strategies and Measures*, http://www.drrteam-dsswater.nl/wp-content/uploads/2015/08/2014dec_myanmarstudy.pdf. [18]

Vreugdenhil, H., B. Hoang and A. Offermans (2012), "Perspectives on Water Management in the Vietnamese Mekong Delta", *Proceedings of The 2nd World Sustainability Forum*, http://dx.doi.org/10.3390/wsf2-00964. [9]

Wagner, F., V. Tran and F. Renaud (2012), "Groundwater Resources in the Mekong Delta: Availability, Utilization and Risks", in *Springer Environmental Science and Engineering, The Mekong Delta System*, Springer Netherlands, Dordrecht, http://dx.doi.org/10.1007/978-94-007-3962-8_7. [21]

WEPA (2015), *WEPA Outlook on Water Environmental Management in Asia*, Water Environmental Partnership in Asia, Japan Ministry of the Environment/Institute for Global Environmental Strategies, Tokyo/Kanagawa, http://www.wepa-db.net/pdf/2015outlook/WEPA_Outlook2015_english.pdf. [16]

WHO (2015), *Country Highlights: Thailand*, UN-Water Global Analysis and Assessment of Sanitation and Drinking Water, World Health Organization, Geneva, http://www.who.int/water_sanitation_health/monitoring/investments/thailand-10-nov-2.pdf?ua=1. [19]

WHO-UN Water (2014), "UN reveals major gaps in water and sanitation – especially in rural areas", WHO UN-Water News release, New York/Geneva, https://www.who.int/news-room/detail/19-11-2014-un-reveals-major-gaps-in-water-and-sanitation-especially-in-rural-areas. [7]

WHO-UNICEF (2017), *Safely Managed Drinking Water: Thematic Report on Drinking Water 2017*, World Health Organization, Geneva, Switzerland, https://data.unicef.org/resources/safely-managed-drinking-water/. [29]

Wilbers, G., Z. Sebesvari and F. Renaud (2014), "Piped-Water Supplies in Rural Areas of the Mekong Delta, Vietnam: Water Quality and Household Perceptions", *Water*, Vol. 6/8, pp. 2175-2194, http://dx.doi.org/10.3390/w6082175. [8]

Willetts, J. et al. (2017), "Good water governance for inclusive growth and poverty reduction", presentation at the 2017 OzWater Conference, Sydney, http://hdl.handle.net/10453/115352. [36]

World Bank (2019), *Vietnam: Toward a Safe, Clean, and Resilient Water System*, World Bank, Washington, DC, http://documents.worldbank.org/curated/en/589341559130979599/pdf/Vietnam-Toward-a-Safe-Clean-and-Resilient-Water-System.pdf. [14]

World Bank (2014), *Vietnam: Review of Urban Water and Wastewater Utility Reform and Regulation*, World Bank, Washington DC, http://documents.worldbank.org/curated/en/886931468125694191/pdf/ACS94240WP0P1496510Box385256B00PUBLIC0.pdf. [20]

World Bank (2014), *Water Supply and Sanitation in Lao PDR*, World Bank, Washington, DC, http://www.wsp.org/sites/wsp/files/publications/WSP-LaoPDR-WSS-Turning-Finance-into-Service-for-the-Future.pdf. [30]

WSP and World Bank (2015), *Water Supply and Sanitation in Cambodia, Turning Finance into Services for the Future*, World Bank, Washington, DC, http://www.wsp.org/sites/wsp/files/publications/WSP-Cambodia-WSS-Turning-Finance-into-Service-for-the-Future.pdf. [42]

WSP and World Bank (2014), *Water Supply and Sanitation in Lao PDR, Turning Finance into Services for the Future*, World Bank, Washington, DC, http://www.wsp.org/sites/wsp/files/publications/WSP-LaoPDR-WSS-Turning-Finance-into-Service-for-the-Future.pdf. [11]

Annex 5.A. Country-specific tables

Annex Table 5.A.1. Cambodia, State of regulatory functions

Regulatory function	State
Tariff regulation	Tariffs need to account for capital and recurrent operation costs of the water system, customer willingness-to-pay, efficiency and simplicity. Many waterworks fail to achieve full cost recovery (2014-2018 NSDP).
Quality standard for drinking water	In line with WHO standards since 2004. Phnom Penh Water Supply Authority regulated by the Ministry of Industry, Mines and Energy. Groundwater shows arsenic contamination. Shortage of physical and human capital for management. Legal framework for consumer recourse is weak.
Quality standard for wastewater treatment	Ministry of Health sets treatment standards. Inadequate institutional and legal frameworks (such as regulation on septic effluent disposal) present problems in urban areas. Poor enforcement in rural areas leads to dumping of waste into water supply despite stronger laws.
Defining technical/industry and service standards	Construction of waterworks requires permits, and co-operation between national and local authorities. Water quality and use quantity plans must be submitted to the Ministry of Water Resources and Meteorology (MOWRAM). Different definitions of usage purpose contribute to drinking water access gap (>97% in Phnom Penh with water piped into dwelling versus <60% elsewhere).
Setting incentives for efficient use of water resources	Cambodia has legislation for Farmers' Water User Communities (FWUC), but only 6.3% of collective irrigation projects have an FWUC. Fewer than half the farmers in communities with FWUC participate, and trust in government and local leaders is low. Public consultation is needed to rebuild the reputation of FWUC.
Promoting innovative technologies	Government provides rewards or grants for research and development, leading to less waste, better water quality or more efficient use.
Promoting demand management	Cambodia lags in this area. Initiatives are poorly developed or absent.
Information and data gathering	WWS data centralised at MOWRAM. Access is free for non-commercial users; commercial users pay a fee. Some information is classified. Collection is infrequent and standardisation of definitions is necessary for compatibility of sources and accurate analysis.
Monitoring of service delivery performance	Apparently absent.
Licensing of water operators	Cambodian Ministry of Industry and Handicraft licenses private water operators. As of 2015, there are an estimated 300 water operators, of which only 147 are licensed. Licensing of the others is ongoing.
Customer engagement	Phnom Penh Water Supply Authority (PPWSA) operates information campaigns. Efforts outside Phnom Penh are uncertain.
Consumer protection and dispute resolution	PPWSA handles complaints, which are recorded and forwarded to the correct departments. Procedures outside of Phnom Penh are uncertain.

Annex Table 5.A.2. Lao PDR, State of regulatory functions

Regulatory function	State
Tariff regulation	Per "Law on Water Supply 2009", regulators set structures, processes and assessments based on end use purpose and user categories. Political considerations prevent increasing low tariffs.
Quality standard for drinking water	Ministry of Health Decree 953 (2003) set standards for 12 indicators, Minister's Decision on Water Quality Standard for Management for Drinking and Domestic Use No. 561/MOH (2014) increases standards to 23 indicators. National Centre of Environmental Health and Water Supply conducts regular sampling and analysis. Reports are mainly written in Lao and difficult to access, impeding proper structural assessment.
Defining technical/industry and service standards	Water supply infrastructure development process is clearly outlined, with well-identified standards for sustainability, construction, equipment and water quality. Roles of ministries are delineated and well-defined.
Setting incentives for efficient investment	Water and sanitation are highly dependent on external funding. Tax and fee breaks encourage involvement, but poor revenue collection and high operating costs are deterrents.
Promoting demand management	Lao PDR lags behind in this area.
Information and data gathering	National Water Supply Data and Information System supports development, monitoring, assessment and implementation of policies and operations.
Monitoring of service delivery performance	Apparently absent.
Licensing of water operators	Requirements to establish water supply operations, and the related investment mechanism, are detailed in the legislation. Responsibilities for each level of government are clearly delegated.
Supervision of contracts with utilities/private actors	Contract supervision is required by legislation. Rights, obligations, term and termination policies are well-defined. Water suppliers are also responsible for sanitation. Fire departments have free access to water.
Supervising utilities' financing activities	Legislation outlines state funding policy and authorisation of the establishment of the Water Supply Development Fund for maintenance, improvement and development of water supply infrastructure. Funding is both public and private. Tax policies include investment relief.
Consumer protection and dispute resolution	Regulation permits filing complaints for unsatisfactory service. Legal channels to address disputes are widespread and strong.

Annex Table 5.A.3. Myanmar, State of regulatory functions

Regulatory function	State
Quality standard for drinking water	Surface water is the primary source for all activities, but Inle Lake (largest source) contains unsafe levels of contaminants from agricultural runoff. Safe drinking water must be piped in from elsewhere, but system is sparse and intakes often unclean.
Quality standard for wastewater treatment	Wastewater treatment regulation is disorganised, with multiple agencies involved. Co-operation among agencies must be improved, within a logic of consolidation. Insufficient treatment infrastructure in urban areas.
Defining technical/industry and service standards	Current legislation requires Ministry of Transport approval for any construction that could affect water resources.
Setting incentives for efficient use of water resources	Government carries out several initiatives to promote and support water conservation, but efforts are hampered by poor irrigation efficiency and lack of incentives to conserve. State-owned irrigation systems do not recover costs.
Information and data gathering	Data are lacking, and the little available data are difficult to access.
Monitoring of service delivery performance	Lacking or not publicly available. Transparency must improve.

Annex Table 5.A.4. Thailand, State of regulatory functions

Regulatory function	State
Tariff regulation	Provincial Waterworks Authority (PWA) sets tariffs. Tariff regulation is barely mentioned in legislation. Drinking water tariffs are based on policies from the 1940s. Wastewater services are free for most of the population.
Quality standard for drinking water	Government is highly involved in the provision of safe drinking water. National standards exist and testing programme by Ministry of Health is extensive and reliable. Further improvements hampered by lack of skilled labour.
Quality standard for wastewater treatment	Regulations set by the Minister of Science, Technology and Environment. Procedures for handling effluent are developed following advice of the Pollution Control Committee and the approval of the National Environment Board, though they are mostly ignored. Water contamination is common.
Defining technical/industry and service standards	National Environment Board can request environmental impact studies of projects. Otherwise, work in this area is limited.
Setting incentives for efficient use of water resources	No incentive schemes and barely any regulations exist. Water security concerns appear to be ignored.
Promoting innovative technologies	Metropolitan Waterworks Authority (MWA) has promoted development and production of water-saving devices and services, including software to detect leaking pipes and a mobile application for consumers to monitor usage.
Promoting demand management	Water conservation awareness is part of compulsory education. The Water Conservation Camp, for example, aims to raise awareness in the value of water and water conservation among students in two river basin areas in the Nonthaburi province. Efforts are also targeted to the general public.
Monitoring of service delivery performance	Apparently absent.
Supervising utilities' financing activities	National Environmental Quality Act delegates responsibility of water management funding to the Environmental Fund. Principles and priorities that must be met to access money from the Fund are well-defined. Remittance of interest income to the Treasury is forbidden.
Customer engagement	"Quality Water for Quality Life" initiative allows customers access to information on service status and both government and do-it-yourself repairs. Feedback can also be given. Outlines of rights and duties in the areas of water and environmental protection exist, but are largely misunderstood or ignored. Further public education is key.
Consumer protection and dispute resolution	Consumers have the right to seek compensation for damages caused by pollution and to report environmental law offenders.

Annex Table 5.A.5. Viet Nam, State of regulatory functions

Regulatory function	State
Tariff regulation	Regulations on tariffs are detailed and water supply companies have financial autonomy. Despite minimum pricing, tariffs remain too low for full cost recovery. A declining collection rate in urban areas exacerbates this problem.
Quality standard for drinking water	Ministry of Health sets standards for water used for drinking or personal hygiene.
Quality standard for wastewater treatment	Discharge of wastewater requires licensing and adherence to quality standards. Despite that, only 10% of wastewater is treated and downstream water quality is poor as a result.
Defining public service obligations/social regulation	Socio-cultural differences including value of water and sanitation practices among ethnic groups with relation to water hamper resource management. Formal studies needed.
Defining technical/industry and service standards	Feasibility studies are undertaken for water infrastructure expansion, and maintenance is a collective effort. Supply companies are responsible for metering. Service quality requirements are well defined and renovation of substandard infrastructure is encouraged.
Setting incentives for efficient use of water resources	Policies exist for assessment, rational exploitation and conservation. However, illegal connections and groundwater contamination remain an issue. Incentives to promote agricultural conservation could be considered.
Setting incentives for efficient investment	Policies promote efficient investments, but only offer incentives to close the urban-rural gap. Projects must be suitable for five years post-commissioning. Feasibility studies must consider life cycle costs.
Promoting innovative technologies	Legislation promotes development and implementation of technologies to address a wide array of issues related to increased demand and declining quality. Korea Smart Water Management is a potential model. Standardisation of parts across regions will simplify maintenance.
Promoting demand management	Vietnamese attitude of water as limitless and God-given makes reform challenging. The Law on Water Resources is an attempt to change this attitude. A shift from fixed to volume-based pricing is under consideration.
Analysing water utilities' investments plans/business plans	Water supply investment must comply with approved construction plans and feasibility studies, and be preceded by public consultation. Excessive decentralisation to water suppliers creates challenges.
Information and data gathering	Information on policies, resources observation, surveillance and various databases is rich, but no longer free to access since 2012.
Monitoring of service delivery performance	Viet Nam is lagging behind in this area.
Licensing of water operators	Licensing of water operators is primarily locally-based, but to a certain extent subject to national plans.
Supervision of contracts with utilities/private actors	Legislation defines contract supervision requirements. Rights and obligations for consumers and suppliers are stated, but compliance enforcement is poor. This discourages investment.
Supervising utilities' financing activities	Apparently absent.
Customer engagement	Ministry of Construction guides public consultation, but participation is limited in practice.
Consumer protection and dispute resolution	Consumers can seek compensation for overcharging, but technology to quantify water losses accurately is lacking.
Advice and advocacy	Both central government and People's Committees have roles in supervision, making it highly inefficient. Non-resident Vietnamese experts are consulted, but expertise within the Ministry of Natural Resources and Environment is limited. Human capital growth in this area is essential.

www.ingramcontent.com/pod-product-compliance
Ingram Content Group UK Ltd.
Pitfield, Milton Keynes, MK11 3LW, UK
UKHW051506290926
15471UKWH00008B/1443